Thinking Tree Books
FunSchooling.com

COPYWORK

Copy a paragraph from one of your books.

TITLE: _____

PAGE NUMBER: _____

MATH TIME
USE YOUR MATH BOOK OR ONLINE MATH PROGRAM
Or be creative and design something, like a house!
You could make graphs, maps or geometric designs with this graph paper.

MY MATH RESOURCE: _____
Please note what math book, video or program you are using today.

Nature Study

Go outside and make a realistic drawing of something you find in nature. Label your drawing.

Reading Time – 1 Hour (Set a Timer)

Choose Four Books - Read from each book for 15 minutes. Copy important words or pictures from each book here:

COPYWORK

Copy a paragraph from one of your books.

TITLE: _____

PAGE NUMBER: _____

_____
_____
_____
_____
_____
_____
_____
_____
_____
_____
_____
_____
_____
_____
_____
_____
_____
_____
_____
_____

Spelling Time Word Hunt

Choose a number between 5 and 12.

#_____

Find 20 words with this many letters.
Write them on this page.

MATH TIME
USE YOUR MATH BOOK OR ONLINE MATH PROGRAM
Or be creative and design something, like a house!
You could make graphs, maps or geometric designs with this graph paper.

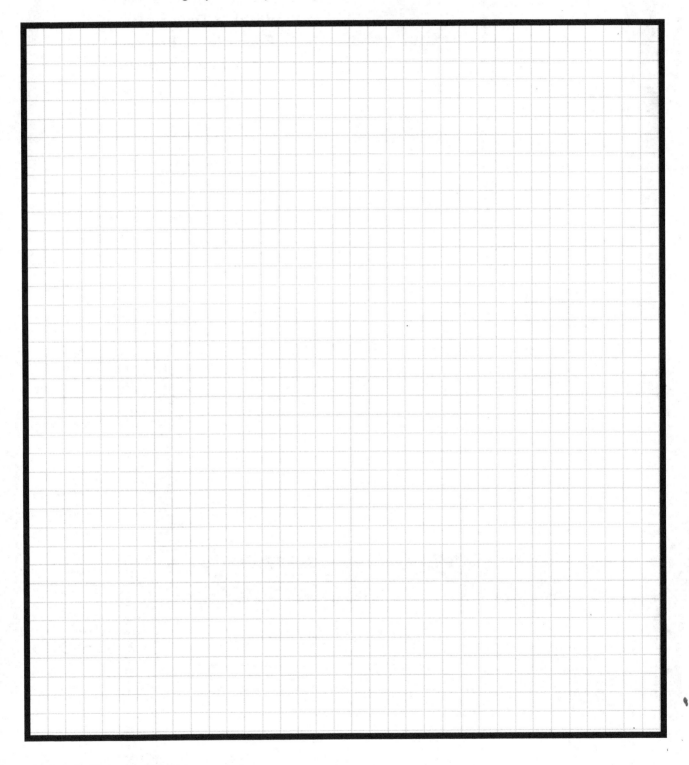

MY MATH RESOURCE: _____
Please note what math book, video or program you are using today.

Date Page - Circle Today's Date

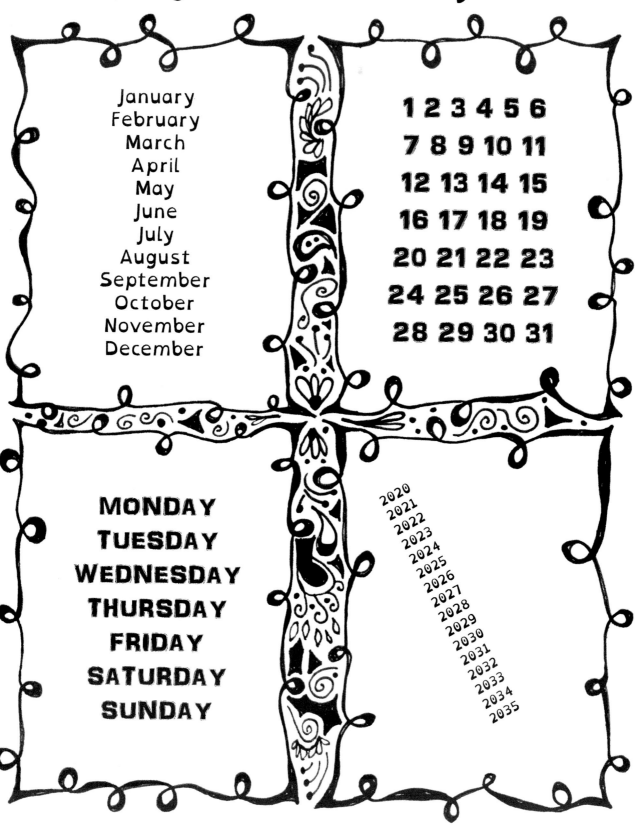

January
February
March
April
May
June
July
August
September
October
November
December

1 2 3 4 5 6
7 8 9 10 11
12 13 14 15
16 17 18 19
20 21 22 23
24 25 26 27
28 29 30 31

MONDAY
TUESDAY
WEDNESDAY
THURSDAY
FRIDAY
SATURDAY
SUNDAY

2020
2021
2022
2023
2024
2025
2026
2027
2028
2029
2030
2031
2032
2033
2034
2035

Write Today's Date:_____

Start Your Day!

Copy a Verse or Quote

I'm Thankful for:

To-Do List

COPYWORK

Copy a paragraph from one of your books.

TITLE: _____

PAGE NUMBER: _____

Spelling Time Word Hunt

Choose a number between 5 and 12.

#_____

Find 20 words with this many letters.
Write them on this page.

_____   _____

_____   _____

_____   _____

_____   _____

_____   _____

_____   _____

_____   _____

_____   _____

_____   _____

_____   _____

MATH TIME
USE YOUR MATH BOOK OR ONLINE MATH PROGRAM
Or be creative and design something, like a house!
You could make graphs, maps or geometric designs with this graph paper.

MY MATH RESOURCE: _____
Please note what math book, video or program you are using today.

Creative Writing

Stories, Poems, Comics and More.
That's what this page is waiting for!

Date Page - Circle Today's Date

January
February
March
April
May
June
July
August
September
October
November
December

1 2 3 4 5 6
7 8 9 10 11
12 13 14 15
16 17 18 19
20 21 22 23
24 25 26 27
28 29 30 31

MONDAY
TUESDAY
WEDNESDAY
THURSDAY
FRIDAY
SATURDAY
SUNDAY

2020
2021
2022
2023
2024
2025
2026
2027
2028
2029
2030
2031
2032
2033
2034
2035

Write Today's Date:_____

Start Your Day!

Copy a Verse or Quote

I'm Thankful for:

To-Do List

Art & Logic Games

46

Creative Writing Time
Write a short story about this picture.

Nature Study

Go outside and make a realistic drawing of something you find in nature. Label your drawing.

Reading Time – 1 Hour (Set a Timer)

**Choose Four Books - Read from each book for 15 minutes.
Copy important words or pictures from each book here:**

COPYWORK

Copy a paragraph from one of your books.

TITLE: _____

PAGE NUMBER: _____

Spelling Time Word Hunt

Choose a number between 5 and 12.

#_____

Find **20** words with this many letters.
Write them on this page.

MATH TIME
USE YOUR MATH BOOK OR ONLINE MATH PROGRAM
Or be creative and design something, like a house!
You could make graphs, maps or geometric designs with this graph paper.

MY MATH RESOURCE: _____
Please note what math book, video or program you are using today.

Creative Writing

Stories, Poems, Comics and More.

That's what this page is waiting for!

PROJECT TIME

Work on a project like art, building, science, cooking or design.

Take photos of your project and tape them to this page.

Date Page - Circle Today's Date

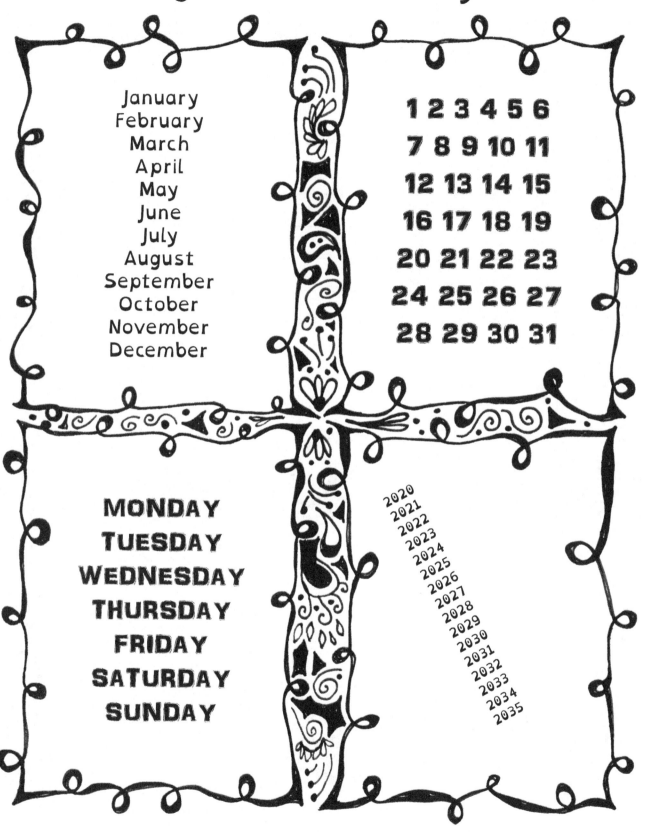

Write Today's Date:_____

Start Your Day!

Copy a Verse or Quote

I'm Thankful for:

To-Do List

Nature Study

Go outside and make a realistic drawing of something you find in nature. Label your drawing.

READING TIME – 1 HOUR (SEt a TIMER)

**Choose Four Books - Read from each book for 15 minutes.
Copy important words or pictures from each book here:**

COPYWORK
Copy a paragraph from one of your books.

TITLE: _____

PAGE NUMBER: _____

_____
_____
_____
_____
_____
_____
_____
_____
_____
_____
_____
_____
_____
_____
_____
_____
_____
_____
_____

MATH TIME
USE YOUR MATH BOOK OR ONLINE MATH PROGRAM
Or be creative and design something, like a house!
You could make graphs, maps or geometric designs with this graph paper.

MY MATH RESOURCE: _____
Please note what math book, video or program you are using today.

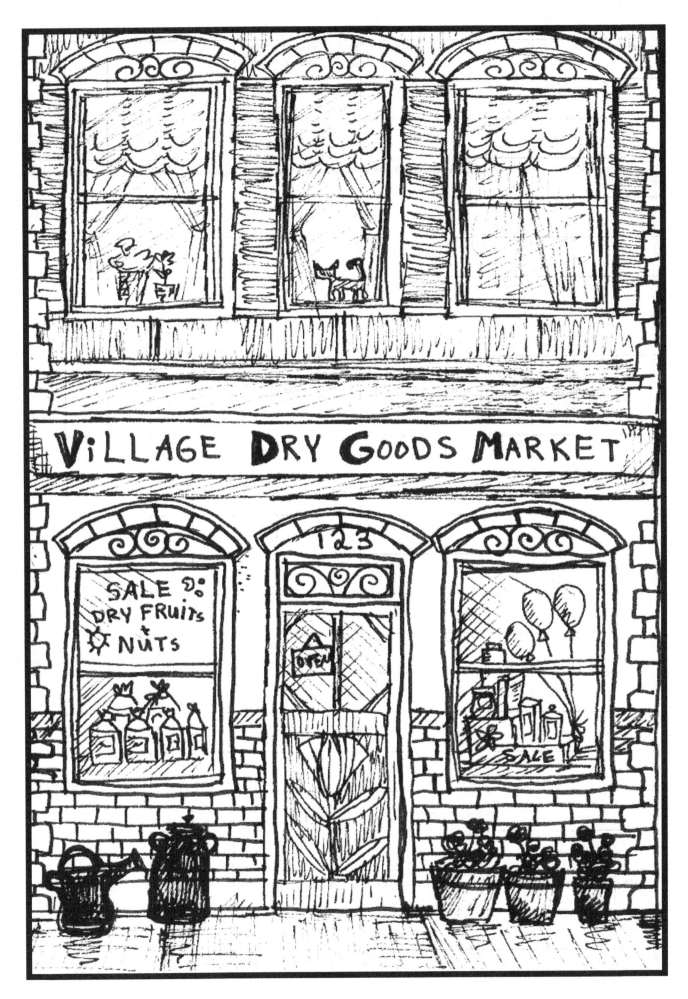

Date Page - Circle Today's Date

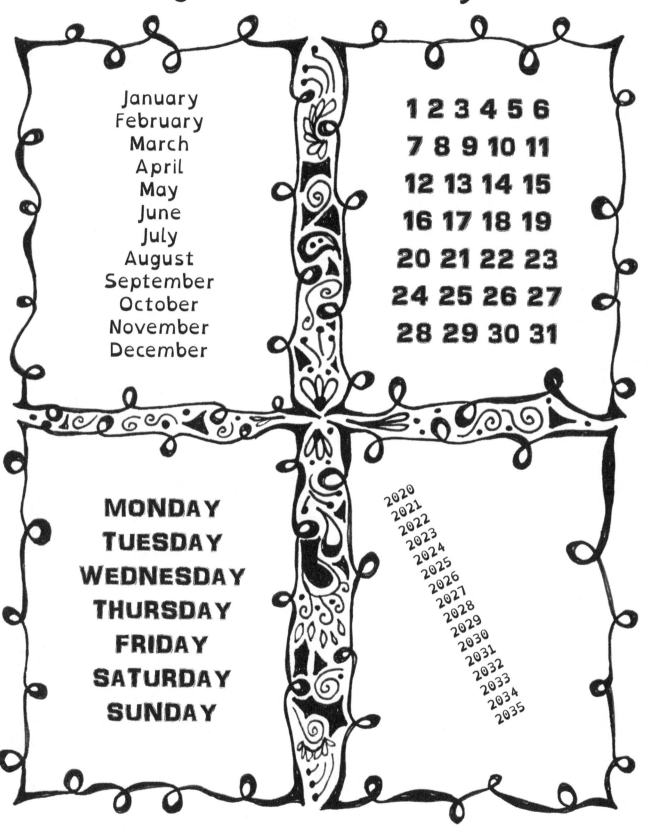

January
February
March
April
May
June
July
August
September
October
November
December

1 2 3 4 5 6
7 8 9 10 11
12 13 14 15
16 17 18 19
20 21 22 23
24 25 26 27
28 29 30 31

MONDAY
TUESDAY
WEDNESDAY
THURSDAY
FRIDAY
SATURDAY
SUNDAY

2020
2021
2022
2023
2024
2025
2026
2027
2028
2029
2030
2031
2032
2033
2034
2035

Write Today's Date:_____

Start Your Day!

Copy a Verse or Quote

I'm Thankful for:

To-Do List

Nature Study
Go outside and make a realistic drawing of something you find in nature. Label your drawing.

Reading Time – 1 Hour (Set a Timer)

Choose Four Books - Read from each book for 15 minutes.
Copy important words or pictures from each book here:

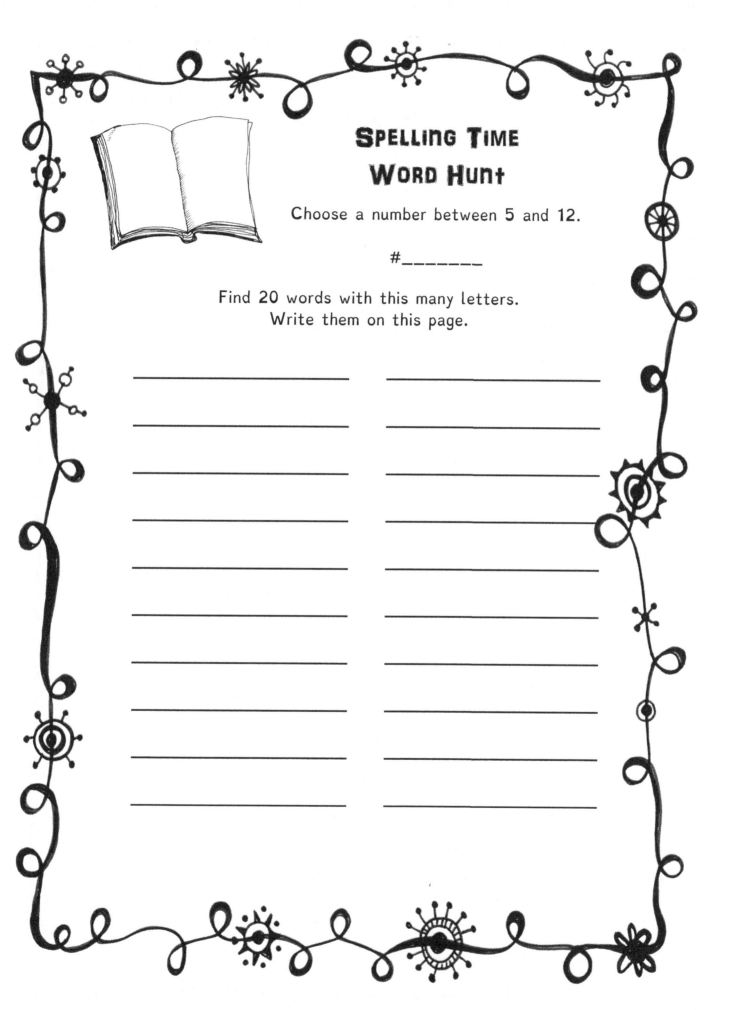

COPYWORK

Copy a paragraph from one of your books.

TITLE: _____

PAGE NUMBER: _____

MATH TIME
USE YOUR MATH BOOK OR ONLINE MATH PROGRAM
Or be creative and design something, like a house!
You could make graphs, maps or geometric designs with this graph paper.

MY MATH RESOURCE: _____
Please note what math book, video or program you are using today.

WORLD NEWS TODAY!

Talk to your parents about current events.
Look at a newspaper, news broadcast or website.
Color the countries you learn about.

CREATE A COMIC STRIP ABOUT TODAY'S NEWS:

Date Page - Circle Today's Date

Write Today's Date: _____

Start Your Day!

Copy a Verse or Quote

I'm Thankful for:

To-Do List

Nature Study

Go outside and make a realistic drawing of something you find in nature. Label your drawing.

Reading Time - 1 Hour (Set a Timer)

Choose Four Books - Read from each book for 15 minutes.
Copy important words or pictures from each book here:

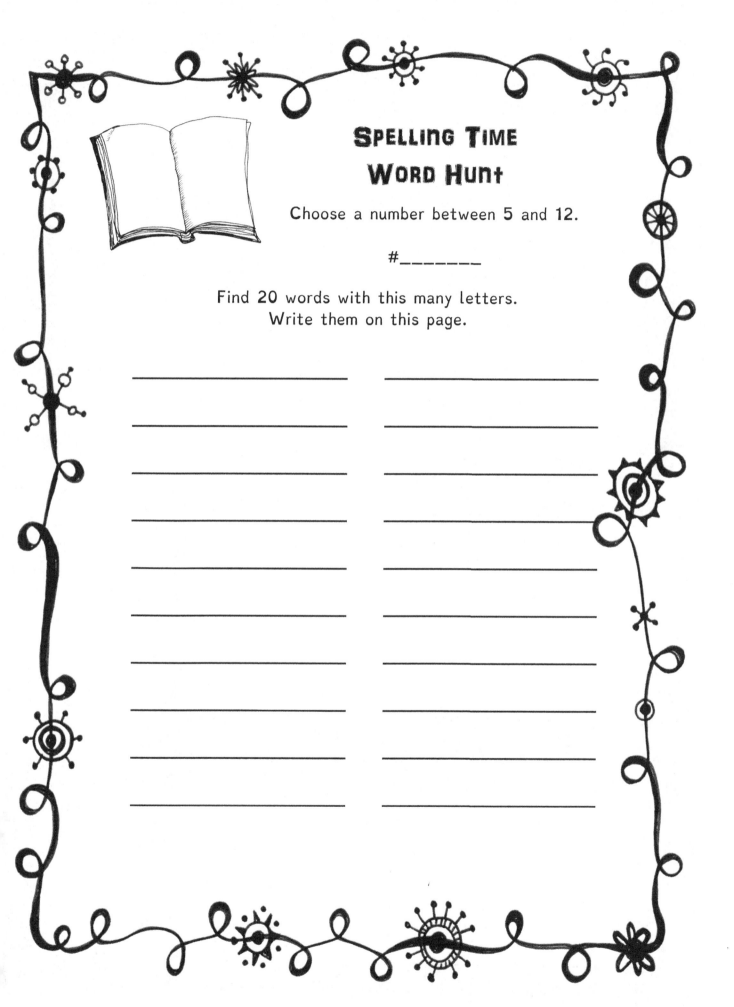

COPYWORK
Copy a paragraph from one of your books.

TITLE: _____

PAGE NUMBER:_____

MATH TIME
USE YOUR MATH BOOK OR ONLINE MATH PROGRAM
Or be creative and design something, like a house!
You could make graphs, maps or geometric designs with this graph paper.

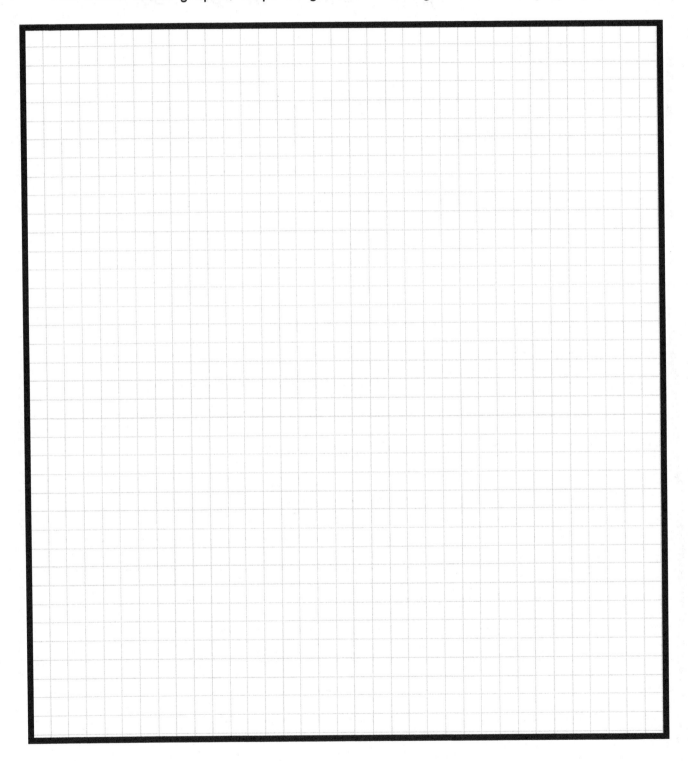

MY MATH RESOURCE: _____
Please note what math book, video or program you are using today.

PROJECT TIME

Work on a project like art, building, science, cooking or design.

Take photos of your project and tape them to this page.

Date Page - Circle Today's Date

January
February
March
April
May
June
July
August
September
October
November
December

1 2 3 4 5 6
7 8 9 10 11
12 13 14 15
16 17 18 19
20 21 22 23
24 25 26 27
28 29 30 31

MONDAY
TUESDAY
WEDNESDAY
THURSDAY
FRIDAY
SATURDAY
SUNDAY

2020
2021
2022
2023
2024
2025
2026
2027
2028
2029
2030
2031
2032
2033
2034
2035

Write Today's Date: _____

Start Your Day!

Copy a Verse or Quote

I'm Thankful for:

To-Do List

Nature Study

Go outside and make a realistic drawing of something you find in nature. Label your drawing.

Reading Time – 1 Hour (Set a Timer)

Choose Four Books - Read from each book for 15 minutes. Copy important words or pictures from each book here:

Spelling Time Word Hunt

Choose a number between 5 and 12.

\#_____

Find 20 words with this many letters.
Write them on this page.

MATH TIME
USE YOUR MATH BOOK OR ONLINE MATH PROGRAM
Or be creative and design something, like a house!
You could make graphs, maps or geometric designs with this graph paper.

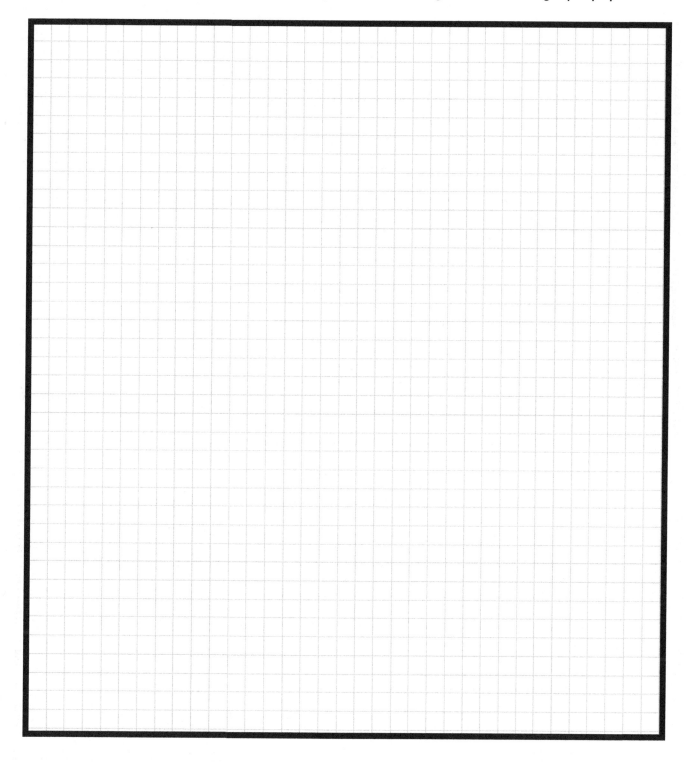

MY MATH RESOURCE: _____
Please note what math book, video or program you are using today.

COPYWORK
Copy a paragraph from one of your books.

TITLE: _____

PAGE NUMBER: _____

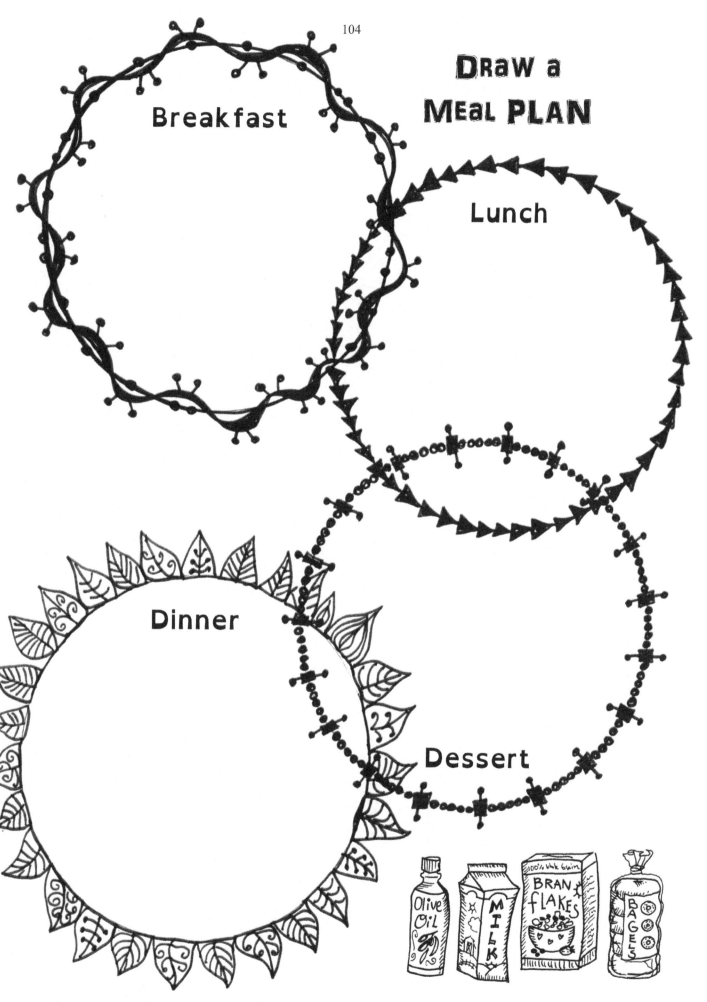

Date Page – Circle Today's Date

Write Today's Date: _____

Start Your Day!

Copy a Verse or Quote

I'm Thankful for:

To-Do List

Nature Study
Go outside and make a realistic drawing of something you find in nature. Label your drawing.

Reading Time – 1 Hour (Set a Timer)

Choose Four Books - Read from each book for 15 minutes.
Copy important words or pictures from each book here:

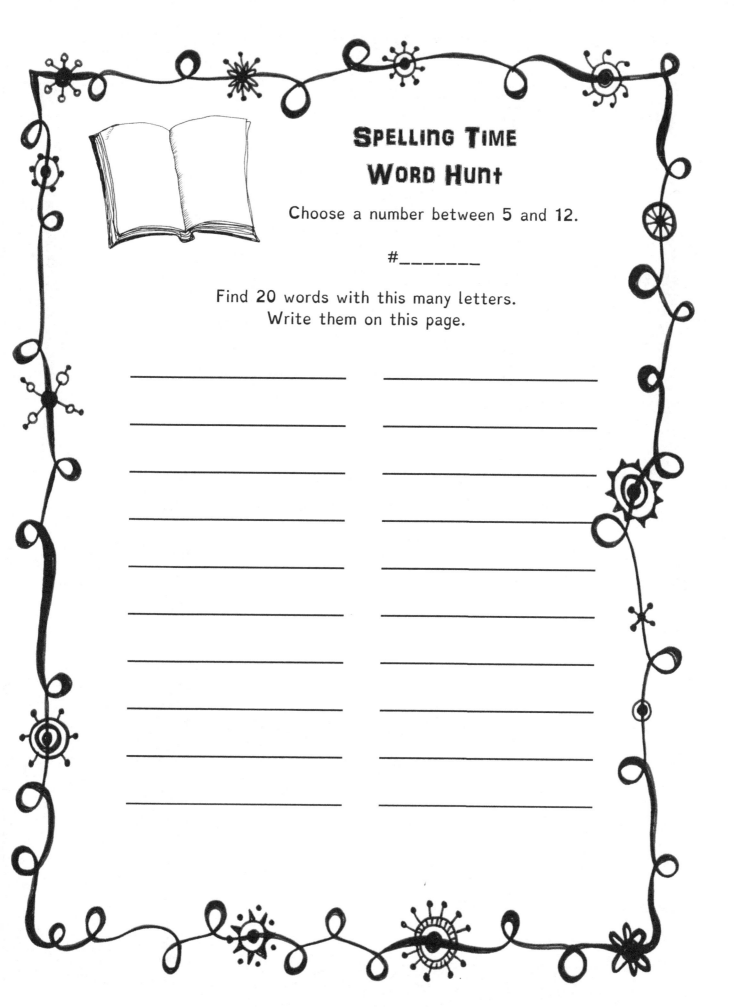

COPYWORK

Copy a paragraph from one of your books.

TITLE: _____

PAGE NUMBER: _____

_____
_____
_____
_____
_____
_____
_____
_____
_____
_____
_____
_____
_____
_____
_____
_____
_____
_____
_____
_____
_____

MATH TIME
USE YOUR MATH BOOK OR ONLINE MATH PROGRAM
Or be creative and design something, like a house!
You could make graphs, maps or geometric designs with this graph paper.

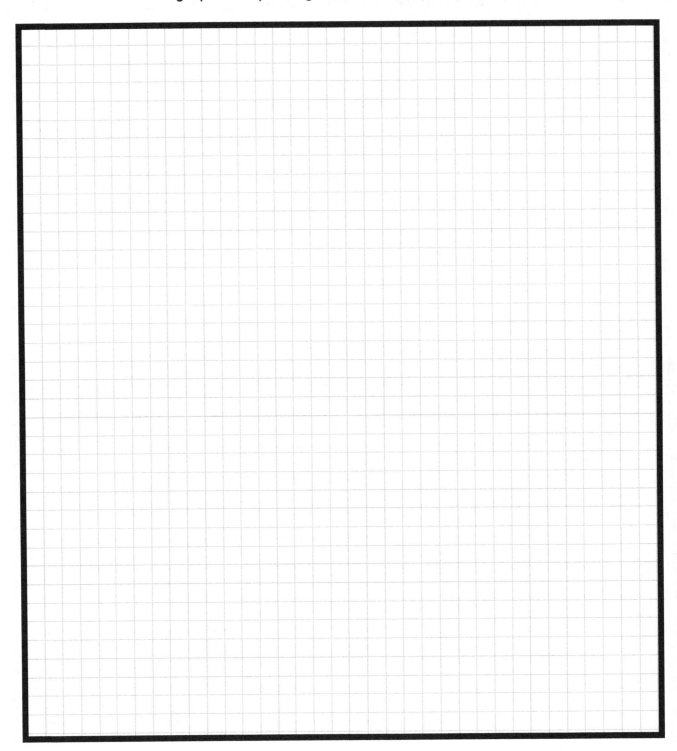

MY MATH RESOURCE: _____
Please note what math book, video or program you are using today.

Creative Writing

Stories, Poems, Comics and More.
That's what this page is waiting for!

Date Page - Circle Today's Date

Write Today's Date: _____

Start Your Day!

Copy a Verse or Quote

I'm Thankful for:

To-Do List

Nature Study

Go outside and make a realistic drawing of something you find in nature. Label your drawing.

Reading Time — 1 Hour (Set a Timer)

Choose Four Books - Read from each book for 15 minutes.
Copy important words or pictures from each book here:

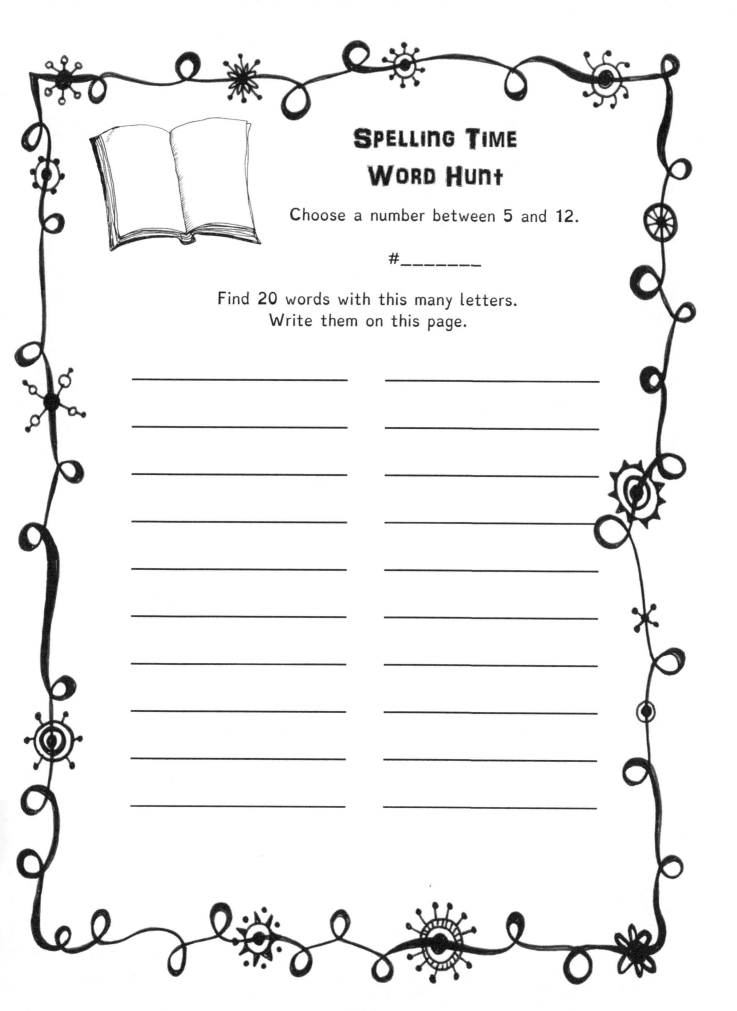

COPYWORK

Copy a paragraph from one of your books.

TITLE: _____

PAGE NUMBER: _____

MATH TIME
USE YOUR MATH BOOK OR ONLINE MATH PROGRAM
Or be creative and design something, like a house!
You could make graphs, maps or geometric designs with this graph paper.

MY MATH RESOURCE: _____
Please note what math book, video or program you are using today.

Creative Writing

Stories, Poems, Comics and More.
That's what this page is waiting for!

Date Page - Circle Today's Date

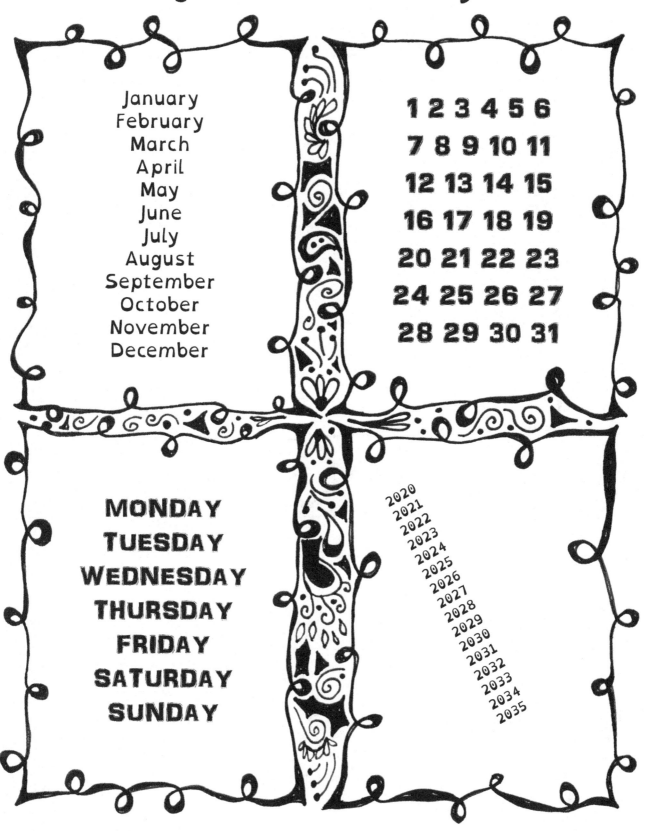

Write Today's Date:_____

Start Your Day!

Copy a Verse or Quote

I'm Thankful For:

To-Do List

Nature Study
Go outside and make a realistic drawing of something you find in nature. Label your drawing.

Reading Time – 1 Hour (Set a Timer)

Choose Four Books - Read from each book for 15 minutes. Copy important words or pictures from each book here:

Spelling Time Word Hunt

Choose a number between 5 and 12.

#_____

Find 20 words with this many letters.
Write them on this page.

MATH TIME
USE YOUR MATH BOOK OR ONLINE MATH PROGRAM
Or be creative and design something, like a house!
You could make graphs, maps or geometric designs with this graph paper.

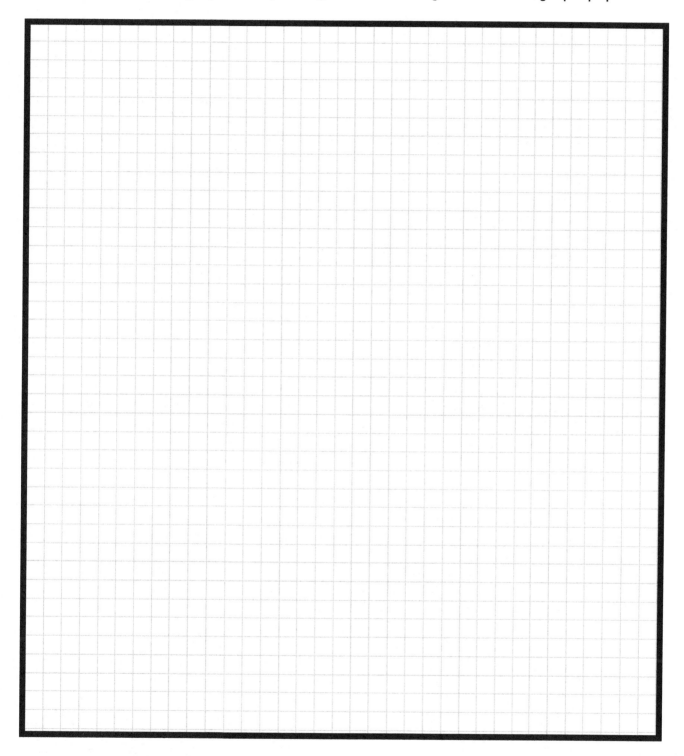

MY MATH RESOURCE: _____
Please note what math book, video or program you are using today.

Creative Writing

Stories, Poems, Comics and More.
That's what this page is waiting for!

Date Page - Circle Today's Date

Write Today's Date: _____

Start Your Day!

COPY A VERSE OR QUOTE

I'M THANKFUL FOR:

TO-DO LIST

Art & Logic Games

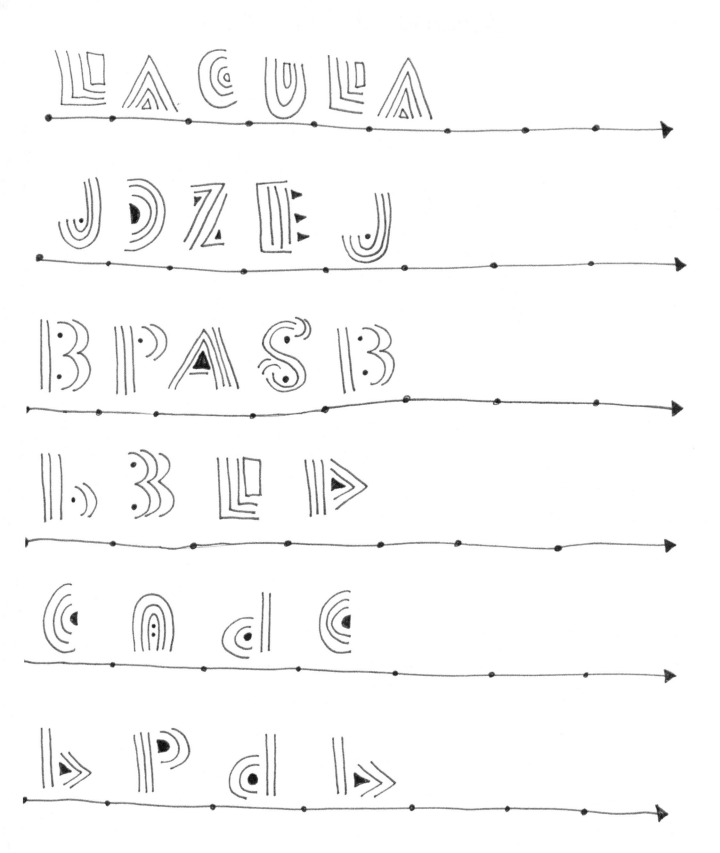

Creative Writing Time
Write a short story about this picture.

Nature Study

Go outside and make a realistic drawing of something you find in nature. Label your drawing.

Reading Time – 1 Hour (Set a Timer)

Choose Four Books – Read from each book for 15 minutes.
Copy important words or pictures from each book here:

Spelling Time Word Hunt

Choose a number between 5 and 12.

#_____

Find **20** words with this many letters.
Write them on this page.

_____   _____
_____   _____
_____   _____
_____   _____
_____   _____
_____   _____
_____   _____
_____   _____
_____   _____
_____   _____

COPYWORK
Copy a paragraph from one of your books.

TITLE: _____

PAGE NUMBER: _____

MATH TIME
USE YOUR MATH BOOK OR ONLINE MATH PROGRAM
Or be creative and design something, like a house!
You could make graphs, maps or geometric designs with this graph paper.

MY MATH RESOURCE: _____
Please note what math book, video or program you are using today.

Date Page - Circle Today's Date

Write Today's Date: _____

Start Your Day!

Copy a Verse or Quote

I'm Thankful For:

To-Do List

Nature Study

Go outside and make a realistic drawing of something you find in nature. Label your drawing.

Reading Time – 1 Hour (Set a Timer)

Choose Four Books – Read from each book for 15 minutes. Copy important words or pictures from each book here:

Spelling Time Word Hunt

Choose a number between 5 and 12.

#_____

Find **20** words with this many letters.
Write them on this page.

_____   _____

_____   _____

_____   _____

_____   _____

_____   _____

_____   _____

_____   _____

_____   _____

_____   _____

_____   _____

MATH TIME
USE YOUR MATH BOOK OR ONLINE MATH PROGRAM
Or be creative and design something, like a house!
You could make graphs, maps or geometric designs with this graph paper.

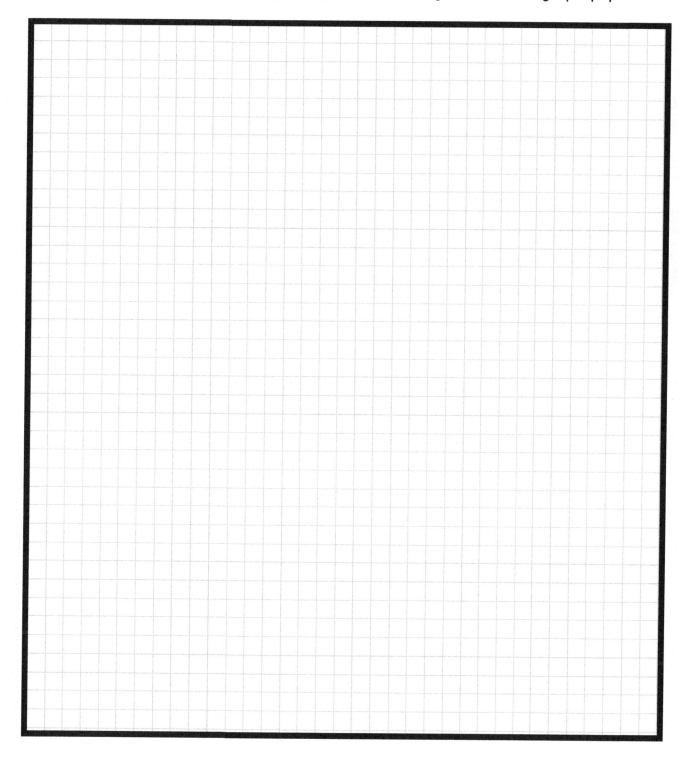

MY MATH RESOURCE: _____
Please note what math book, video or program you are using today.

COPYWORK

Copy a paragraph from one of your books.

TITLE: _____

PAGE NUMBER: _____

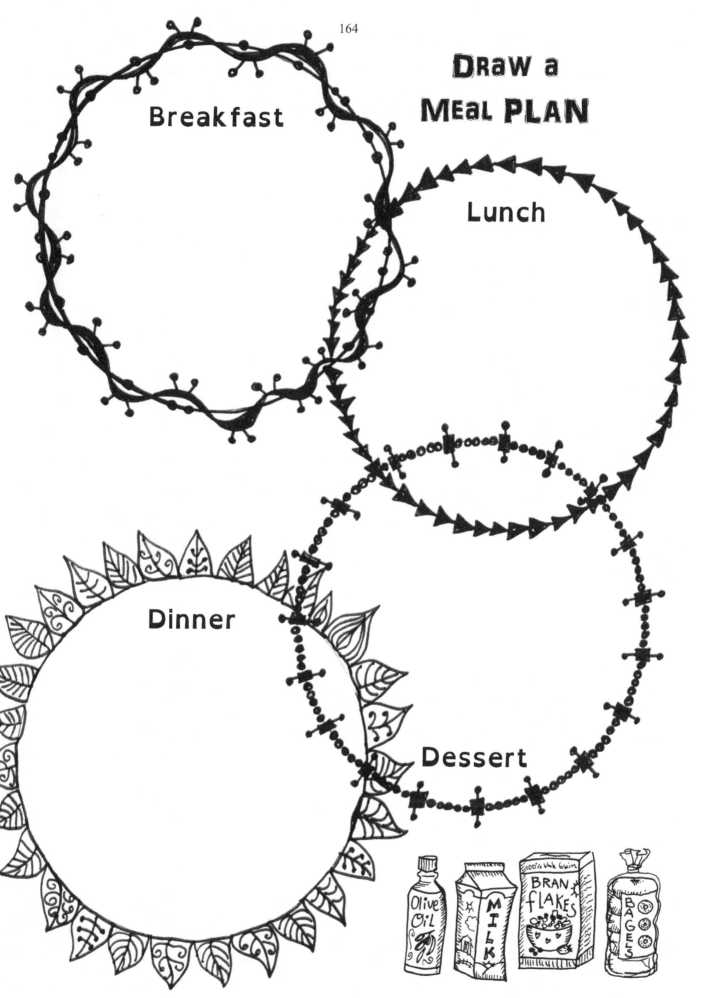

PROJECT TIME

Work on a project like art, building, science, cooking or design.

Take photos of your project and tape them to this page.

Date Page - Circle Today's Date

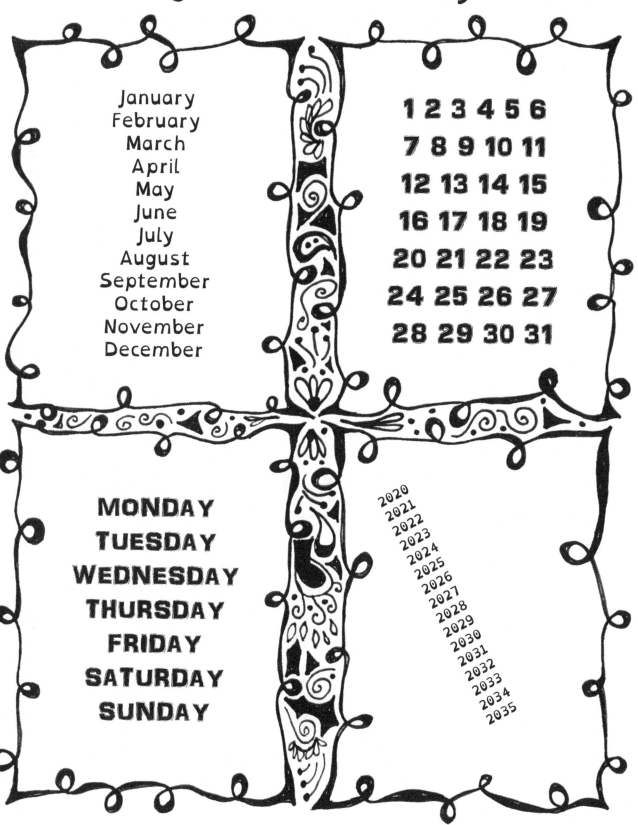

January
February
March
April
May
June
July
August
September
October
November
December

1 2 3 4 5 6
7 8 9 10 11
12 13 14 15
16 17 18 19
20 21 22 23
24 25 26 27
28 29 30 31

MONDAY
TUESDAY
WEDNESDAY
THURSDAY
FRIDAY
SATURDAY
SUNDAY

2020
2021
2022
2023
2024
2025
2026
2027
2028
2029
2030
2031
2032
2033
2034
2035

Write Today's Date:_____

Start Your Day!

Copy a Verse or Quote

I'm Thankful for:

To-Do List

Art & Logic Games

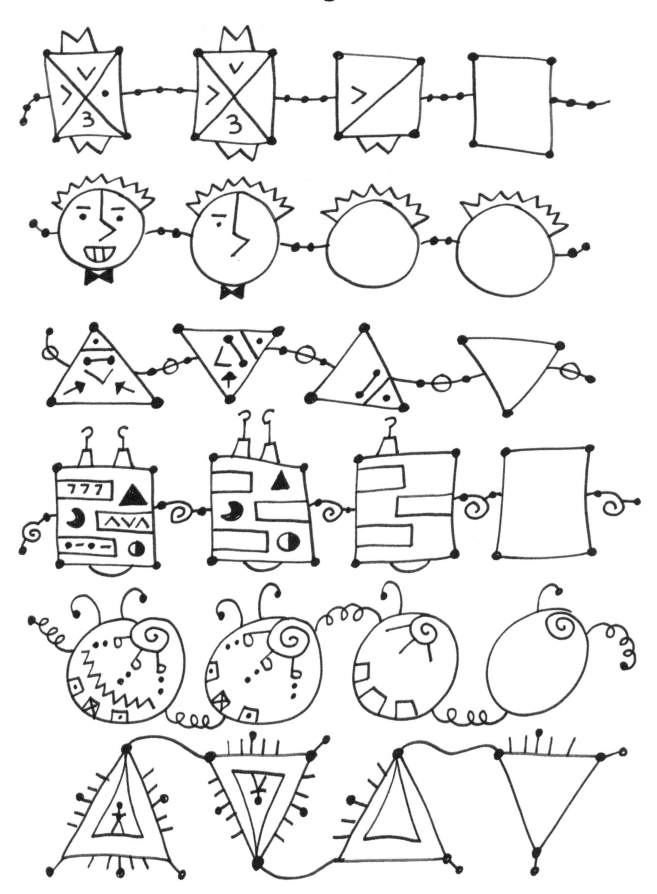

CREATiVE WRiTiNG TiME
Write a short story about this picture.

_____
_____
_____
_____
_____
_____
_____

Nature Study

Go outside and make a realistic drawing of something you find in nature. Label your drawing.

Reading Time – 1 Hour (Set a Timer)

Choose Four Books - Read from each book for 15 minutes. Copy important words or pictures from each book here:

Spelling Time Word Hunt

Choose a number between 5 and 12.

#_____

Find 20 words with this many letters.
Write them on this page.

_____   _____

_____   _____

_____   _____

_____   _____

_____   _____

_____   _____

_____   _____

_____   _____

_____   _____

_____   _____

COPYWORK
Copy a paragraph from one of your books.

TITLE: _____

PAGE NUMBER: _____

MATH TIME
USE YOUR MATH BOOK OR ONLINE MATH PROGRAM
Or be creative and design something, like a house!
You could make graphs, maps or geometric designs with this graph paper.

MY MATH RESOURCE: _____
Please note what math book, video or program you are using today.

Creative Writing

Stories, Poems, Comics and More.
That's what this page is waiting for!

Date Page - Circle Today's Date

January
February
March
April
May
June
July
August
September
October
November
December

1 2 3 4 5 6
7 8 9 10 11
12 13 14 15
16 17 18 19
20 21 22 23
24 25 26 27
28 29 30 31

MONDAY
TUESDAY
WEDNESDAY
THURSDAY
FRIDAY
SATURDAY
SUNDAY

2020
2021
2022
2023
2024
2025
2026
2027
2028
2029
2030
2031
2032
2033
2034
2035

Write Today's Date:_____

Start Your Day!

Copy a Verse or Quote

I'm Thankful for:

To-Do List

Art & Logic Games

CREATIVE WRITING TIME
Write a short story about this picture.

Reading Time – 1 Hour (Set a Timer)

**Choose Four Books - Read from each book for 15 minutes.
Copy important words or pictures from each book here:**

Spelling Time Word Hunt

Choose a number between 5 and 12.

#_____

Find **20** words with this many letters.
Write them on this page.

COPYWORK

Copy a paragraph from one of your books.

TITLE: _____

PAGE NUMBER: _____

MATH TIME
USE YOUR MATH BOOK OR ONLINE MATH PROGRAM
Or be creative and design something, like a house!
You could make graphs, maps or geometric designs with this graph paper.

MY MATH RESOURCE: _____
Please note what math book, video or program you are using today.

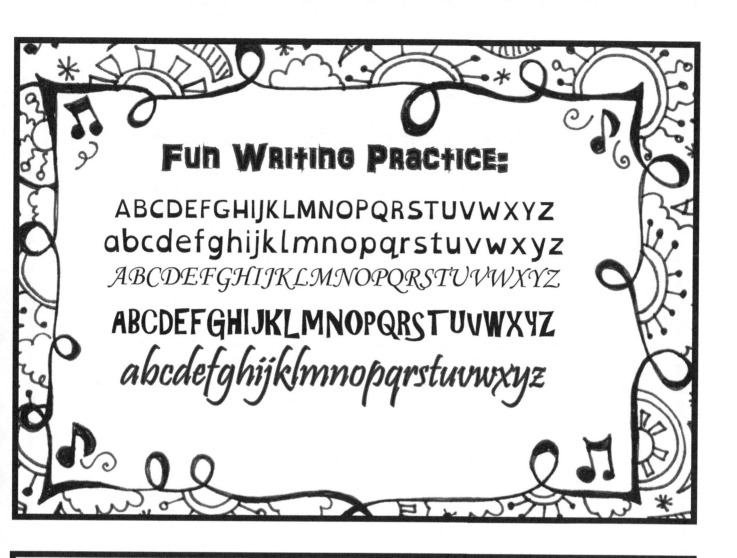

Creative Writing

Stories, Poems, Comics and More.
That's what this page is waiting for!

Date Page - Circle Today's Date

January
February
March
April
May
June
July
August
September
October
November
December

1 2 3 4 5 6
7 8 9 10 11
12 13 14 15
16 17 18 19
20 21 22 23
24 25 26 27
28 29 30 31

MONDAY
TUESDAY
WEDNESDAY
THURSDAY
FRIDAY
SATURDAY
SUNDAY

2020
2021
2022
2023
2024
2025
2026
2027
2028
2029
2030
2031
2032
2033
2034
2035

Write Today's Date:_____

Start Your Day!

Copy a Verse or Quote

I'm Thankful for:

To-Do List

Art & Logic Games

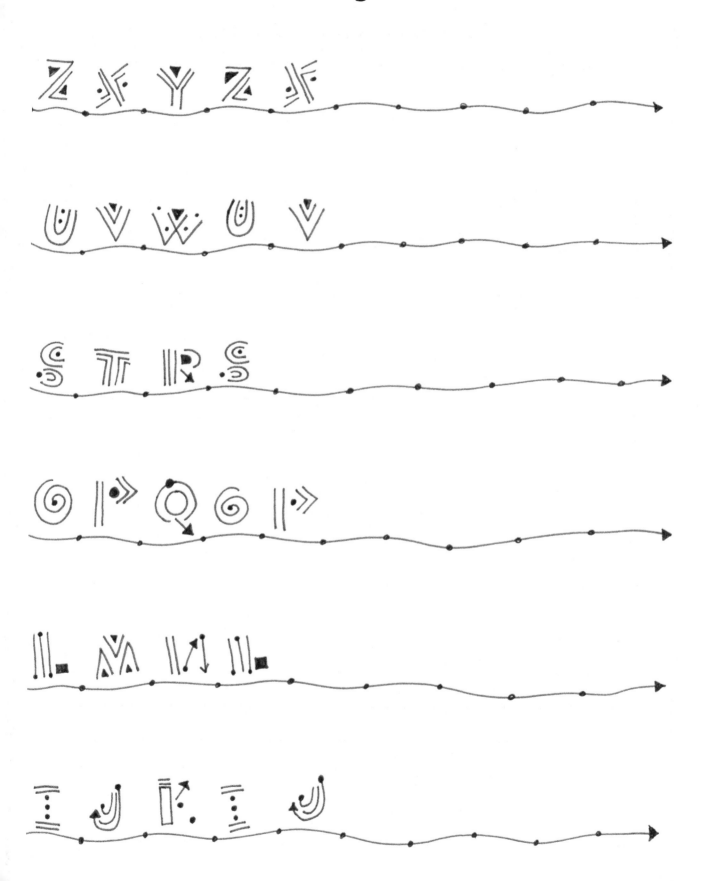

Creative Writing Time
Write a short story about this picture.

Nature Study

Go outside and make a realistic drawing of something you find in nature. Label your drawing.

Reading Time – 1 Hour (Set a Timer)

Choose Four Books - Read from each book for 15 minutes. Copy important words or pictures from each book here:

Spelling Time Word Hunt

Choose a number between 5 and 12.

#_____

Find 20 words with this many letters.
Write them on this page.

_____   _____

_____   _____

_____   _____

_____   _____

_____   _____

_____   _____

_____   _____

_____   _____

_____   _____

_____   _____

MATH TIME
USE YOUR MATH BOOK OR ONLINE MATH PROGRAM
Or be creative and design something, like a house!
You could make graphs, maps or geometric designs with this graph paper.

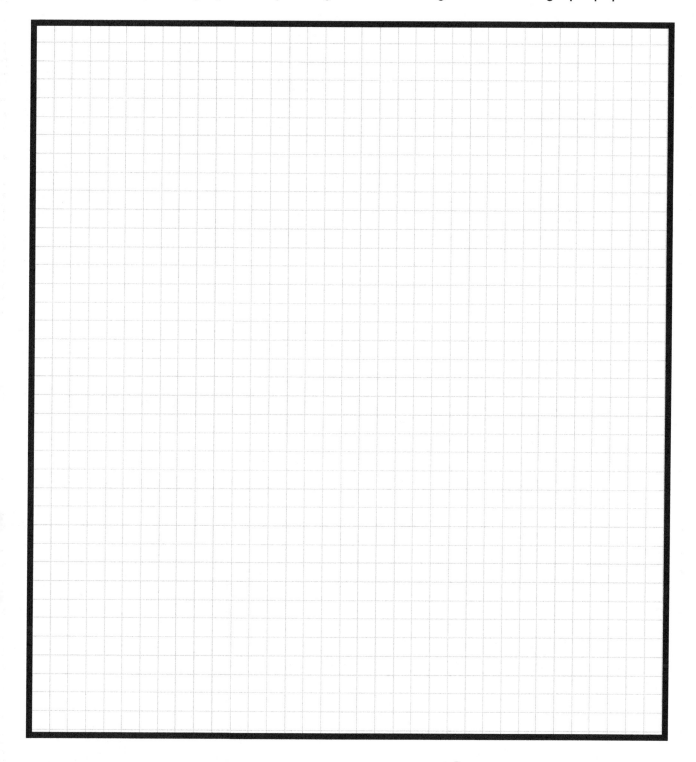

MY MATH RESOURCE: _____
Please note what math book, video or program you are using today.

WORLD NEWS TODAY!

Talk to your parents about current events.
Look at a newspaper, news broadcast or website.
Color the countries you learn about.

CREATE A COMIC STRIP ABOUT TODAY'S NEWS:

Creative Writing

Stories, Poems, Comics and More.
That's what this page is waiting for!

Date Page - Circle Today's Date

Write Today's Date:_____

Start Your Day!

Nature Study

Go outside and make a realistic drawing of something you find in nature. Label your drawing.

Reading Time – 1 Hour (Set a Timer)

Choose Four Books - Read from each book for 15 minutes. Copy important words or pictures from each book here:

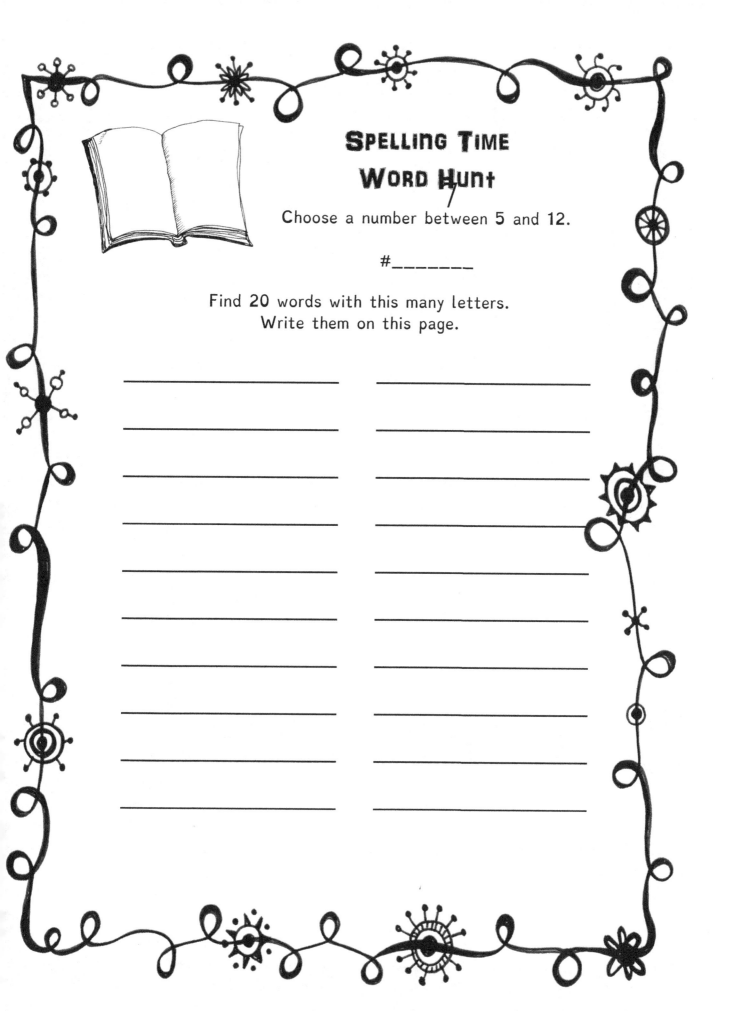

COPYWORK

Copy a paragraph from one of your books.

TITLE: _____

PAGE NUMBER: _____

MATH TIME
USE YOUR MATH BOOK OR ONLINE MATH PROGRAM
Or be creative and design something, like a house!
You could make graphs, maps or geometric designs with this graph paper.

MY MATH RESOURCE: _____
Please note what math book, video or program you are using today.

Date Page - Circle Today's Date

Write Today's Date:_____

Start Your Day!

Art & Logic Games

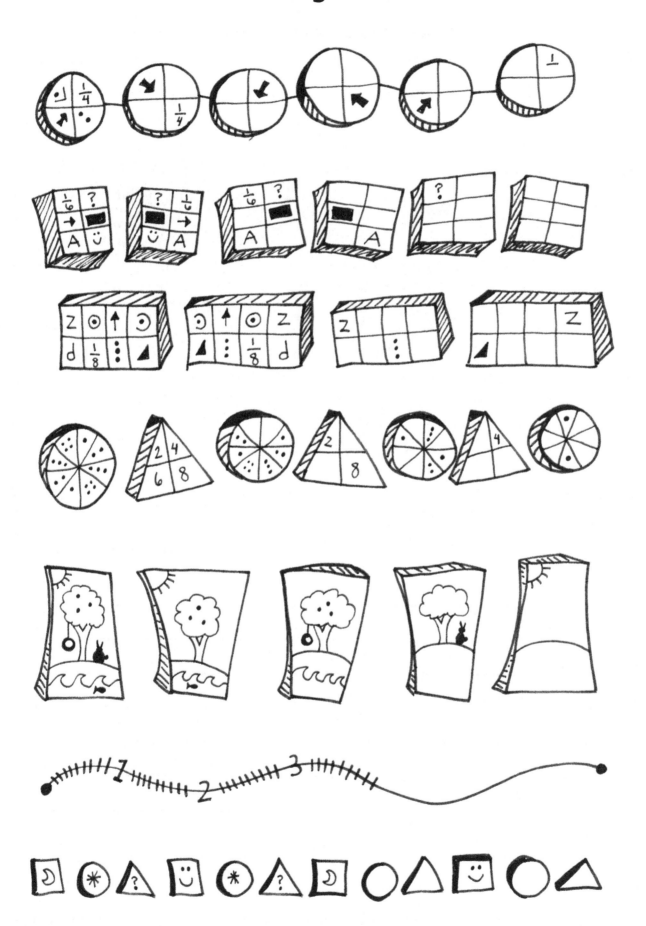

Creative Writing Time
Write a short story about this picture.

Nature Study

Go outside and make a realistic drawing of something you find in nature. Label your drawing.

Reading Time – 1 Hour (Set a Timer)

**Choose Four Books - Read from each book for 15 minutes.
Copy important words or pictures from each book here:**

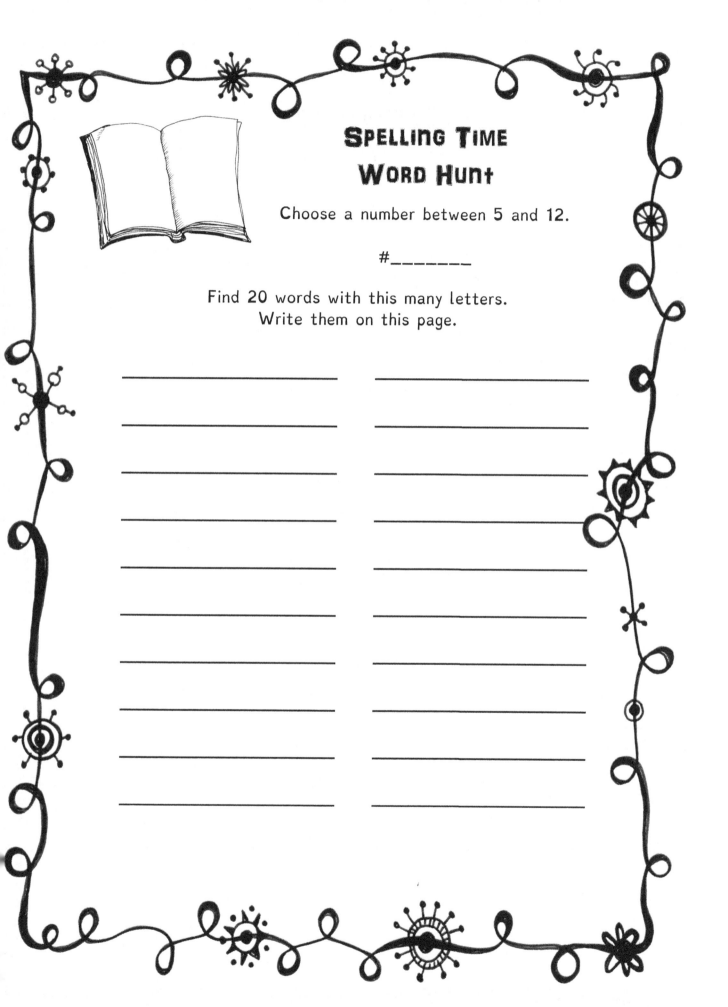

Spelling Time Word Hunt

Choose a number between 5 and 12.

#_____

Find **20** words with this many letters.
Write them on this page.

COPYWORK

Copy a paragraph from one of your books.

TITLE: _____

PAGE NUMBER: _____

MATH TIME
USE YOUR MATH BOOK OR ONLINE MATH PROGRAM
Or be creative and design something, like a house!
You could make graphs, maps or geometric designs with this graph paper.

MY MATH RESOURCE: _____
Please note what math book, video or program you are using today.

Listening Time

Listen to an audio book or classical music or ask someone to read a story to you while you color and draw on the next page.

What are you listening to?

_____

Date Page - Circle Today's Date

Write Today's Date: _____

Start Your Day!

Copy a Verse or Quote

I'm Thankful for:

To-Do List

Art & Logic Games

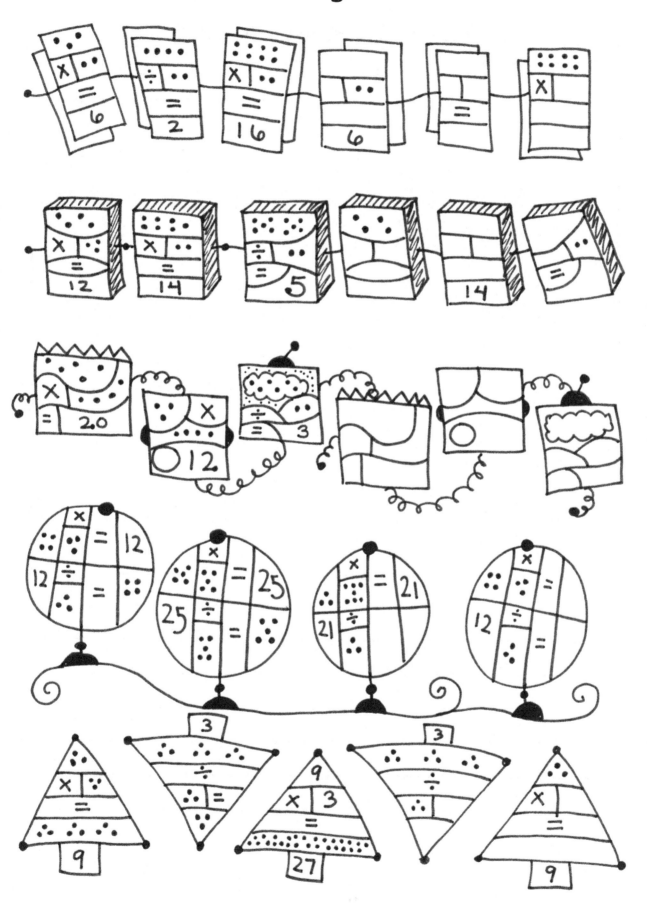

Creative Writing Time
Write a short story about this picture.

Nature Study
Go outside and make a realistic drawing of something you find in nature. Label your drawing.

Reading Time – 1 Hour (Set a Timer)

Choose Four Books - Read from each book for 15 minutes.
Copy important words or pictures from each book here:

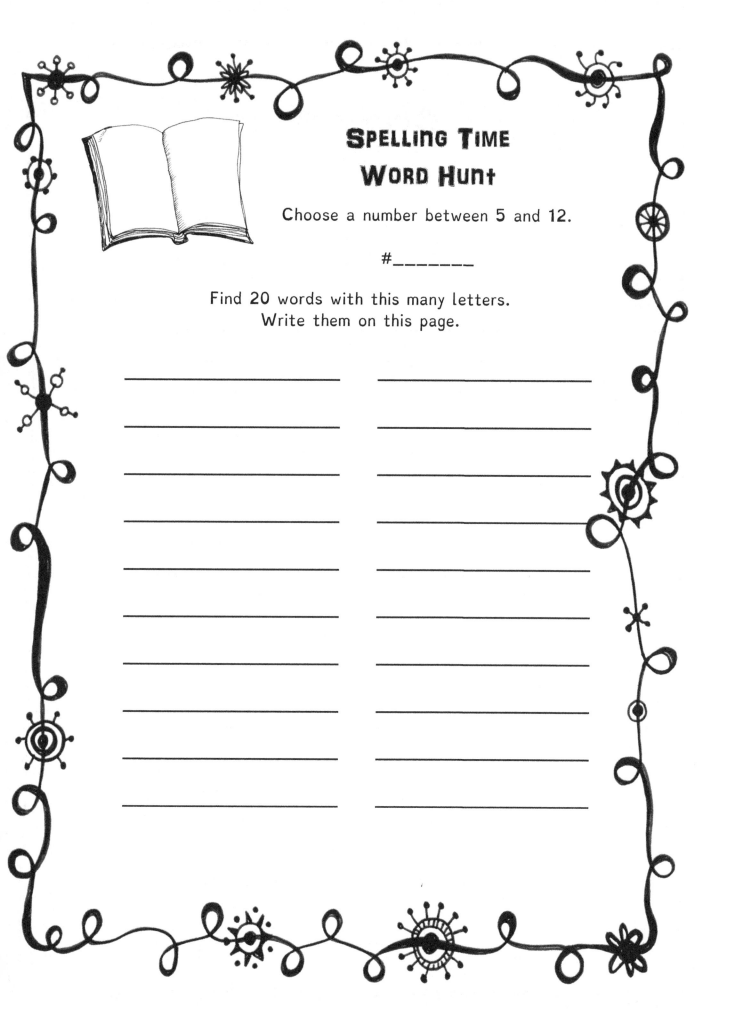

COPYWORK
Copy a paragraph from one of your books.

TITLE: _____

PAGE NUMBER: _____

_____
_____
_____
_____
_____
_____
_____
_____
_____
_____
_____
_____
_____
_____
_____
_____
_____
_____
_____

MATH TIME
USE YOUR MATH BOOK OR ONLINE MATH PROGRAM
Or be creative and design something, like a house!
You could make graphs, maps or geometric designs with this graph paper.

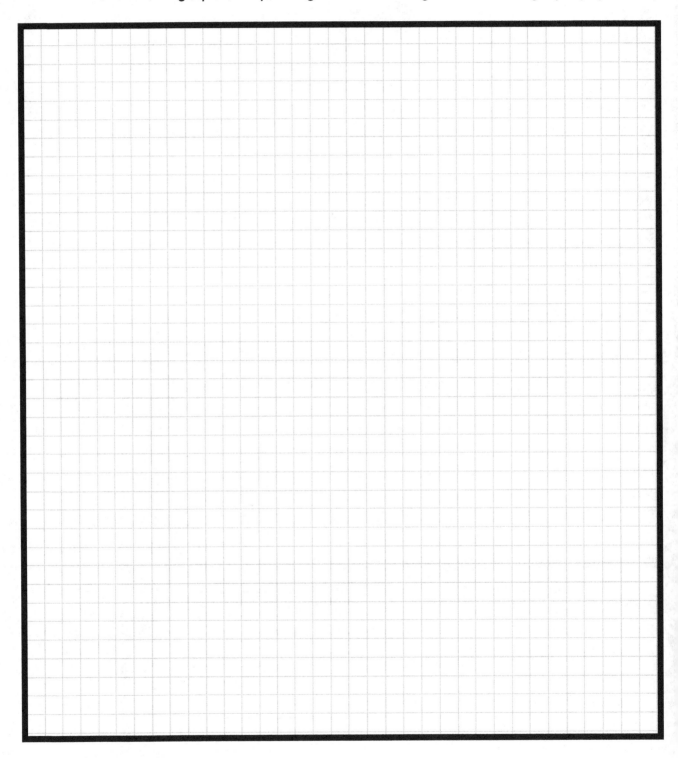

MY MATH RESOURCE: _____
Please note what math book, video or program you are using today.

Creative Writing

Stories, Poems, Comics and More.

That's what this page is waiting for!

Date Page - Circle Today's Date

Write Today's Date:_____

Start Your Day!

Copy a Verse or Quote

I'm Thankful for:

To-Do List

Art & Logic Games

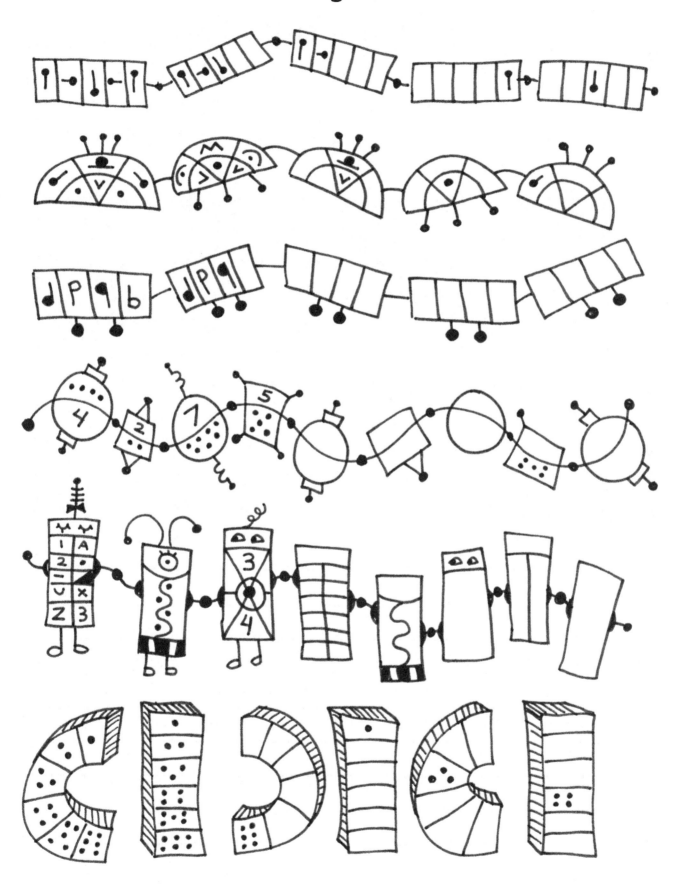

Creative Writing Time
Write a short story about this picture.

Nature Study

Go outside and make a realistic drawing of something you find in nature. Label your drawing.

Reading Time – 1 Hour (Set a Timer)

Choose Four Books - Read from each book for 15 minutes.
Copy important words or pictures from each book here:

Spelling Time Word Hunt

Choose a number between 5 and 12.

#_____

Find 20 words with this many letters.
Write them on this page.

_____   _____

_____   _____

_____   _____

_____   _____

_____   _____

_____   _____

_____   _____

_____   _____

_____   _____

_____   _____

MATH TIME
USE YOUR MATH BOOK OR ONLINE MATH PROGRAM
Or be creative and design something, like a house!
You could make graphs, maps or geometric designs with this graph paper.

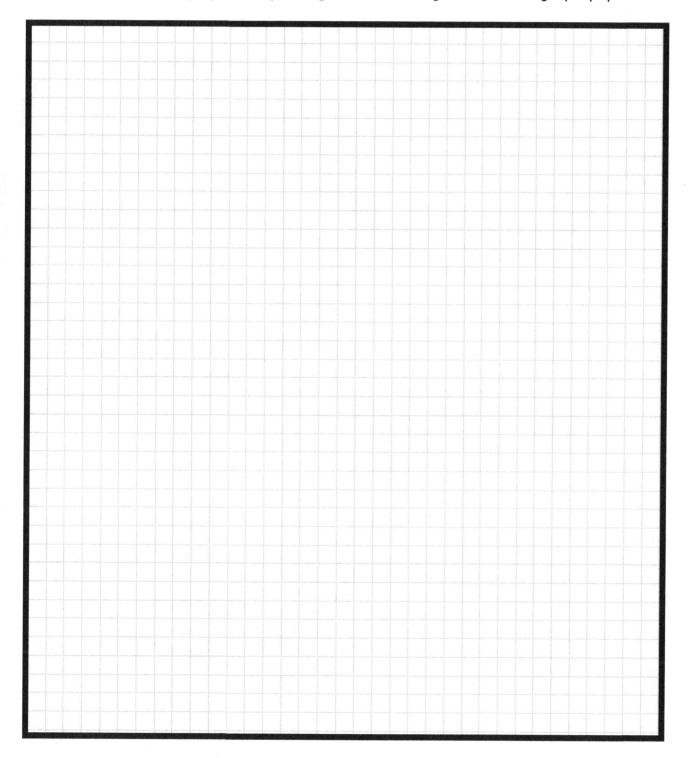

MY MATH RESOURCE: _____
Please note what math book, video or program you are using today.

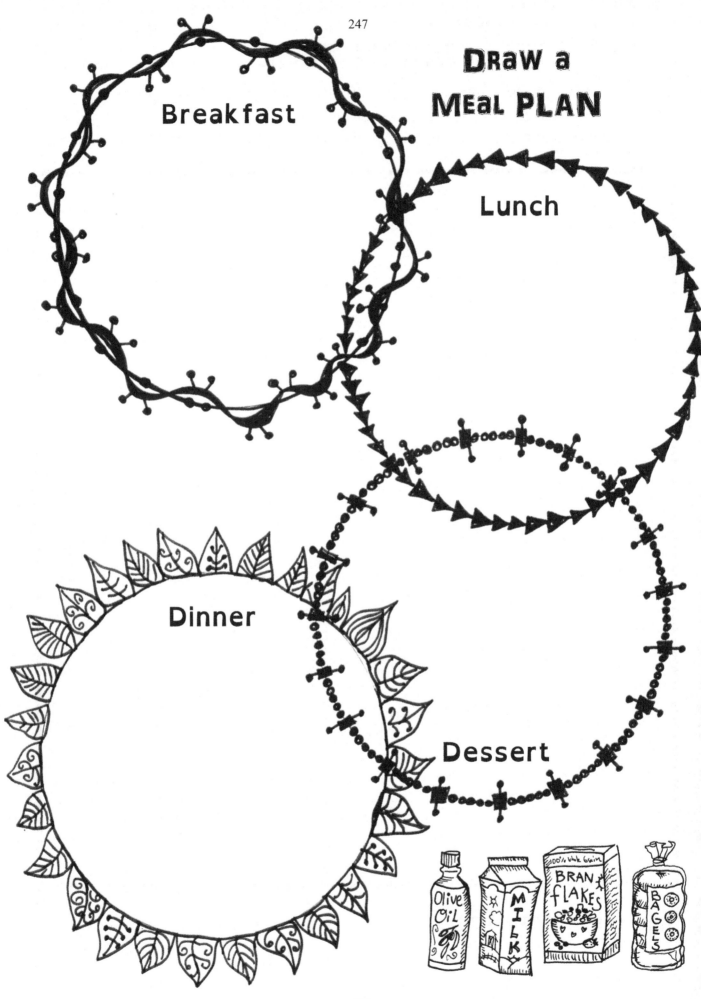

Creative Writing

Stories, Poems, Comics and More.
That's what this page is waiting for!

Date Page - Circle Today's Date

Write Today's Date:_____

Start Your Day!

Copy a Verse or Quote

I'm Thankful for:

To-Do List

Creative Writing Time
Write a short story about this picture.

_____
_____
_____
_____
_____
_____
_____

Nature Study
Go outside and make a realistic drawing of something you find in nature. Label your drawing.

Reading Time — 1 Hour (Set a Timer)

Choose Four Books - Read from each book for 15 minutes.
Copy important words or pictures from each book here:

Spelling Time Word Hunt

Choose a number between 5 and 12.

#_____

Find 20 words with this many letters.
Write them on this page.

_____   _____
_____   _____
_____   _____
_____   _____
_____   _____
_____   _____
_____   _____
_____   _____
_____   _____
_____   _____

COPYWORK
Copy a paragraph from one of your books.

TITLE: _____

PAGE NUMBER: _____

_____
_____
_____
_____
_____
_____
_____
_____
_____
_____
_____
_____
_____
_____
_____
_____
_____
_____
_____
_____
_____

MATH TIME
USE YOUR MATH BOOK OR ONLINE MATH PROGRAM
Or be creative and design something, like a house!
You could make graphs, maps or geometric designs with this graph paper.

MY MATH RESOURCE: _____
Please note what math book, video or program you are using today.

Animal Quiz

How much do you know about this animal?
Can you draw the animal's habitat, food and enemies?

Creative Writing

Stories, Poems, Comics and More.

That's what this page is waiting for!

Start Your Day!

Copy a Verse or Quote

I'm Thankful for:

To-Do List

Creative Writing Time
Write a short story about this picture.

Reading Time – 1 Hour (Set a Timer)

Choose Four Books - Read from each book for 15 minutes. Copy important words or pictures from each book here:

Spelling Time Word Hunt

Choose a number between 5 and 12.

#_____

Find **20** words with this many letters.
Write them on this page.

MATH TIME
USE YOUR MATH BOOK OR ONLINE MATH PROGRAM
Or be creative and design something, like a house!
You could make graphs, maps or geometric designs with this graph paper.

MY MATH RESOURCE: _____
Please note what math book, video or program you are using today.

Animal Quiz

How much do you know about this animal?
Can you draw the animal's habitat, food and enemies?

Creative Writing

Stories, Poems, Comics and More.

That's what this page is waiting for!

Date Page - Circle Today's Date

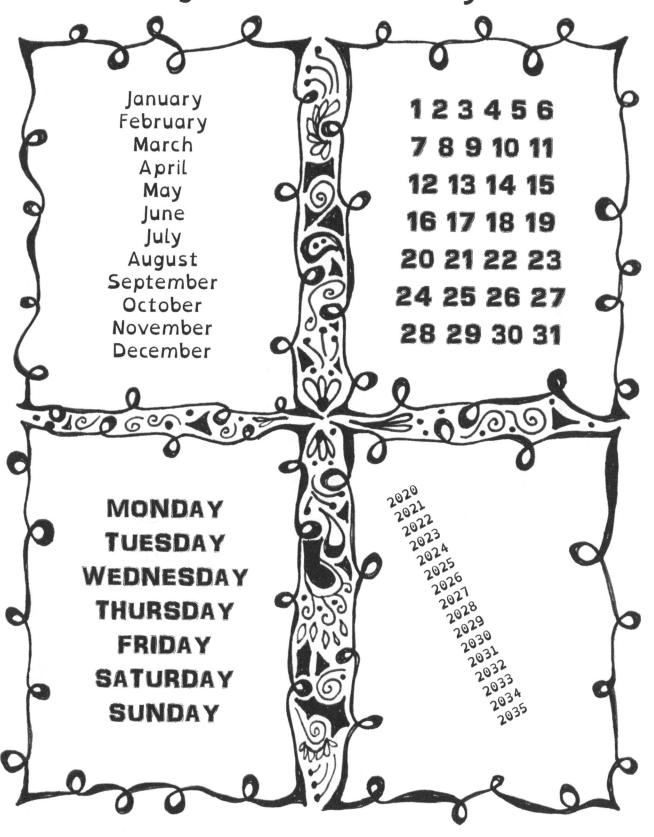

January
February
March
April
May
June
July
August
September
October
November
December

1 2 3 4 5 6
7 8 9 10 11
12 13 14 15
16 17 18 19
20 21 22 23
24 25 26 27
28 29 30 31

MONDAY
TUESDAY
WEDNESDAY
THURSDAY
FRIDAY
SATURDAY
SUNDAY

2020
2021
2022
2023
2024
2025
2026
2027
2028
2029
2030
2031
2032
2033
2034
2035

Write Today's Date:_____

Start Your Day!

Nature Study

Go outside and make a realistic drawing of something you find in nature. Label your drawing.

Reading Time – 1 Hour (Set a Timer)

Choose Four Books - Read from each book for 15 minutes.
Copy important words or pictures from each book here:

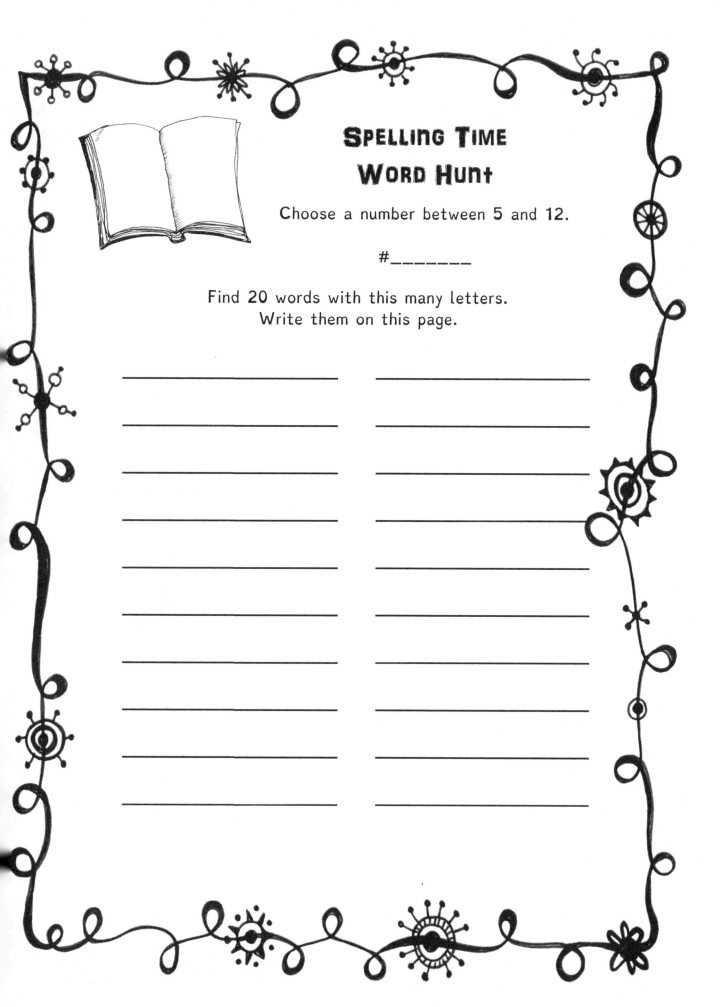

SPELLING TIME WORD HUNT

Choose a number between 5 and 12.

#_____

Find **20** words with this many letters.
Write them on this page.

MATH TIME
USE YOUR MATH BOOK OR ONLINE MATH PROGRAM
Or be creative and design something, like a house!
You could make graphs, maps or geometric designs with this graph paper.

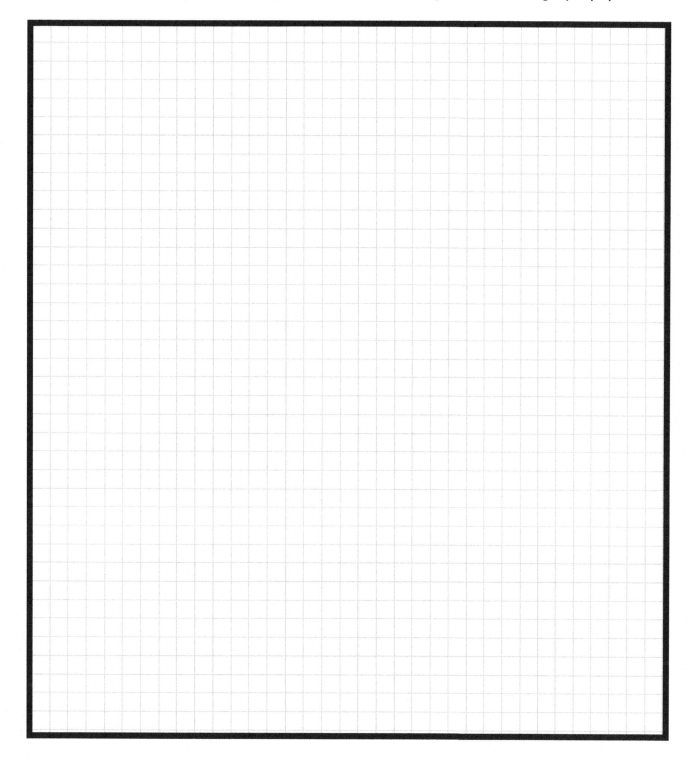

MY MATH RESOURCE: _____
Please note what math book, video or program you are using today.

Animal Quiz

How much do you know about this animal?
Can you draw the animal's habitat, food and enemies?

PROJECT TIME

Work on a project like art, building, science, cooking or design.

Take photos of your project and tape them to this page.

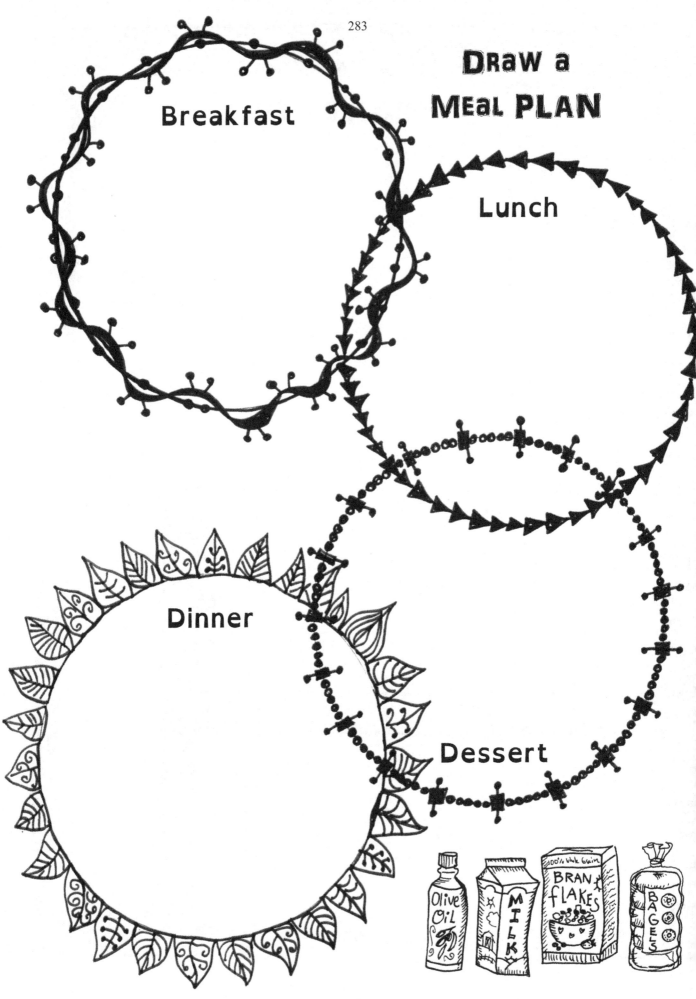

Date Page - Circle Today's Date

January
February
March
April
May
June
July
August
September
October
November
December

1 2 3 4 5 6
7 8 9 10 11
12 13 14 15
16 17 18 19
20 21 22 23
24 25 26 27
28 29 30 31

MONDAY
TUESDAY
WEDNESDAY
THURSDAY
FRIDAY
SATURDAY
SUNDAY

2020
2021
2022
2023
2024
2025
2026
2027
2028
2029
2030
2031
2032
2033
2034
2035

Write Today's Date: _____

Start Your Day!

Copy a Verse or Quote

I'm Thankful for:

To-Do List

Art & Logic Games

Creative Writing Time
Write a short story about this picture.

Nature Study

Go outside and make a realistic drawing of something you find in nature. Label your drawing.

Reading Time – 1 Hour (Set a Timer)

Choose Four Books - Read from each book for 15 minutes. Copy important words or pictures from each book here:

Animal Quiz

How much do you know about this animal?
Can you draw the animal's habitat, food and enemies?

COPYWORK

Copy a paragraph from one of your books.

TITLE: _____

PAGE NUMBER: _____

MATH TIME
Use Your Math Book or Online Math Program
Or be creative and design something, like a house!
You could make graphs, maps or geometric designs with this graph paper.

My Math Resource: _____
Please note what math book, video or program you are using today.

Creative Writing

Stories, Poems, Comics and More.

That's what this page is waiting for!

Date Page - Circle Today's Date

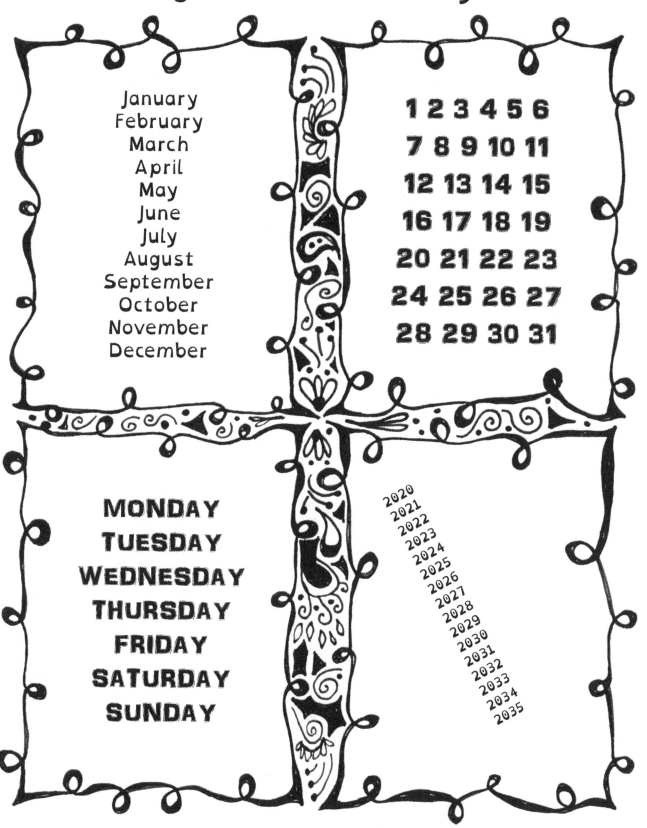

Write Today's Date:_____

Start Your Day!

Copy a Verse or Quote

I'm Thankful for:

To-Do List

Art & Logic Games

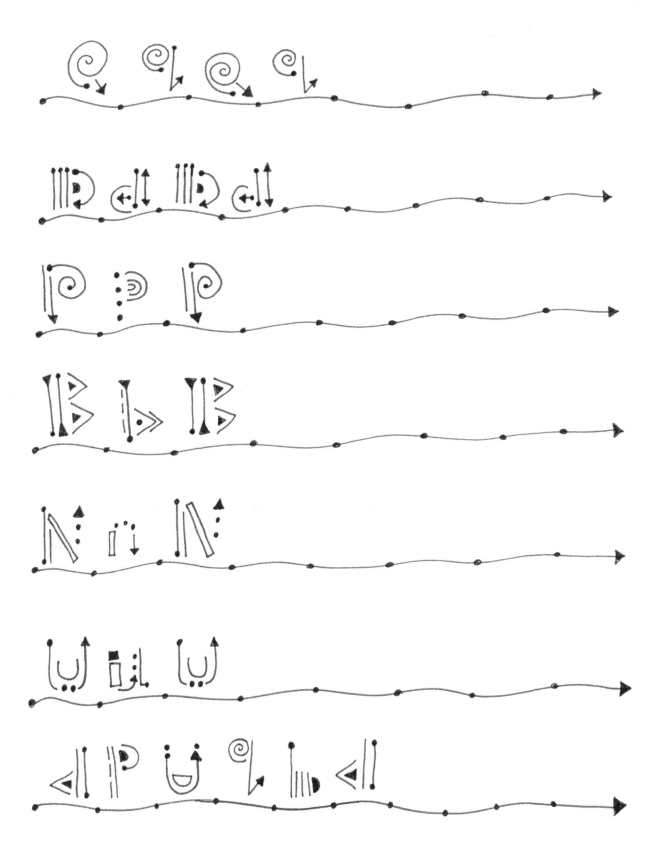

Creative Writing Time
Write a short story about this picture.

Nature Study

Go outside and make a realistic drawing of something you find in nature. Label your drawing.

Reading Time – 1 Hour (Set a Timer)

**Choose Four Books - Read from each book for 15 minutes.
Copy important words or pictures from each book here:**

Spelling Time Word Hunt

Choose a number between 5 and 12.

#_____

Find **20** words with this many letters.
Write them on this page.

_____   _____

_____   _____

_____   _____

_____   _____

_____   _____

_____   _____

_____   _____

_____   _____

_____   _____

_____   _____

MATH TIME
USE YOUR MATH BOOK OR ONLINE MATH PROGRAM
Or be creative and design something, like a house!
You could make graphs, maps or geometric designs with this graph paper.

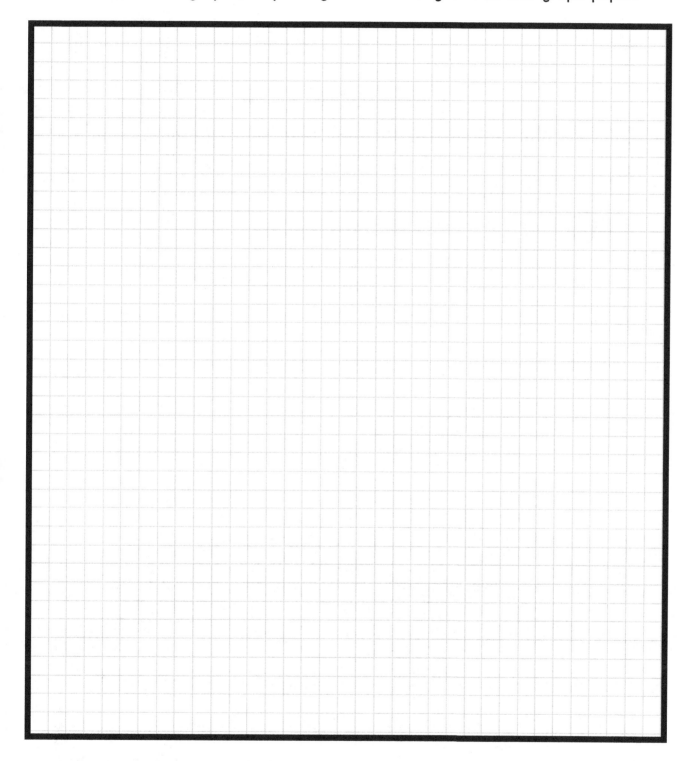

MY MATH RESOURCE: _____
Please note what math book, video or program you are using today.

LISTENING TIME

Listen to an audio book or classical music or ask someone to read a story to you while you color and draw on the next page.

What are you listening to?

_____

Creative Writing

Stories, Poems, Comics and More.
That's what this page is waiting for!

Date Page – Circle Today's Date

January
February
March
April
May
June
July
August
September
October
November
December

1 2 3 4 5 6
7 8 9 10 11
12 13 14 15
16 17 18 19
20 21 22 23
24 25 26 27
28 29 30 31

MONDAY
TUESDAY
WEDNESDAY
THURSDAY
FRIDAY
SATURDAY
SUNDAY

2020
2021
2022
2023
2024
2025
2026
2027
2028
2029
2030
2031
2032
2033
2034
2035

Write Today's Date: _____

Start Your Day!

Copy a Verse or Quote

I'm Thankful for:

To-Do List

Art & Logic Games

CREATIVE WRITING TIME
Write a short story about this picture.

Nature Study

Go outside and make a realistic drawing of something you find in nature. Label your drawing.

Reading Time – 1 Hour (Set a Timer)

Choose Four Books - Read from each book for 15 minutes.
Copy important words or pictures from each book here:

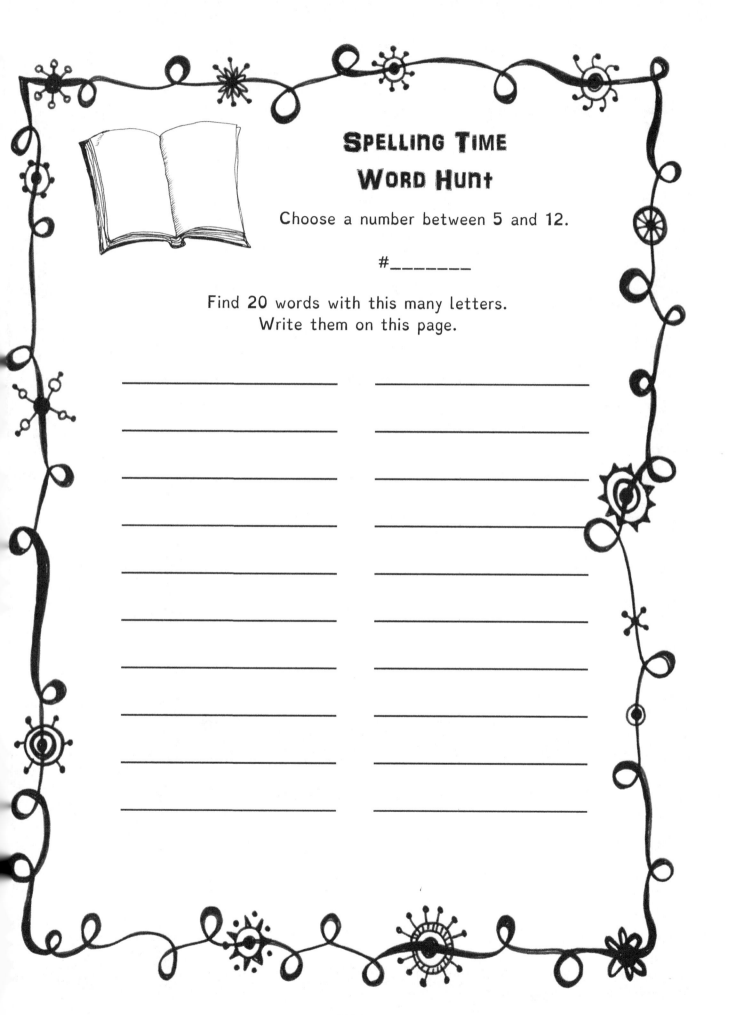

MATH TIME
USE YOUR MATH BOOK OR ONLINE MATH PROGRAM
Or be creative and design something, like a house!
You could make graphs, maps or geometric designs with this graph paper.

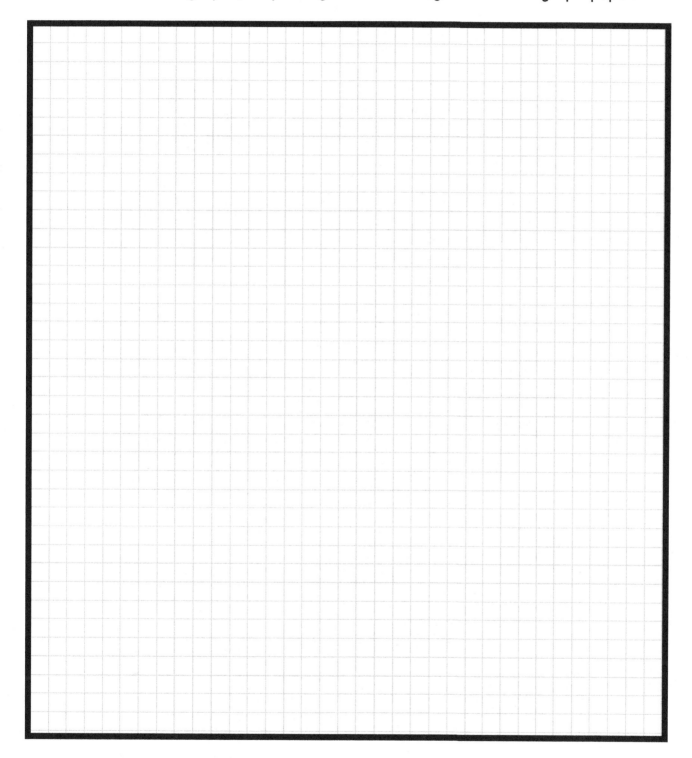

MY MATH RESOURCE: _____
Please note what math book, video or program you are using today.

Animal Quiz

How much do you know about this animal?
Can you draw the animal's habitat, food and enemies?

Creative Writing

Stories, Poems, Comics and More.

That's what this page is waiting for!

Date Page - Circle Today's Date

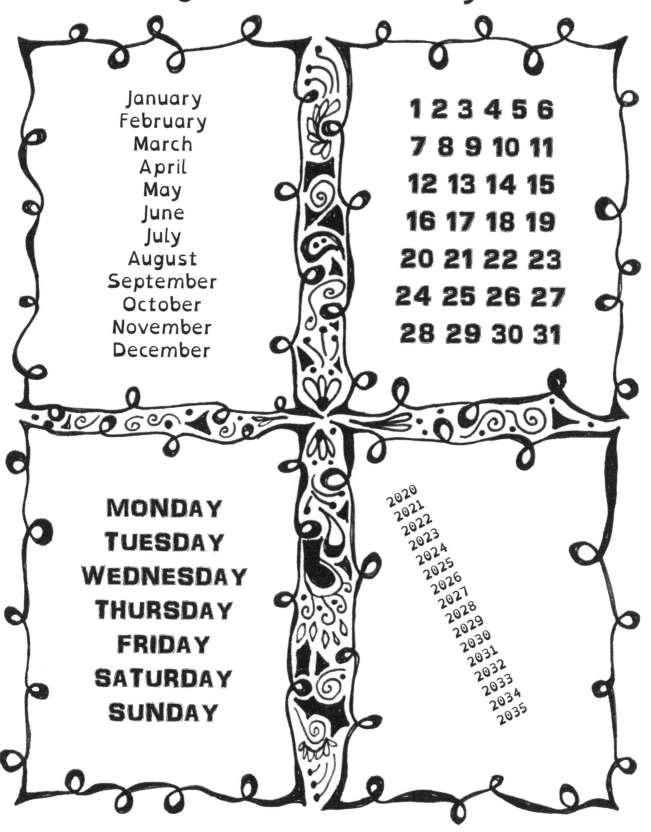

January
February
March
April
May
June
July
August
September
October
November
December

1 2 3 4 5 6
7 8 9 10 11
12 13 14 15
16 17 18 19
20 21 22 23
24 25 26 27
28 29 30 31

MONDAY
TUESDAY
WEDNESDAY
THURSDAY
FRIDAY
SATURDAY
SUNDAY

2020
2021
2022
2023
2024
2025
2026
2027
2028
2029
2030
2031
2032
2033
2034
2035

Write Today's Date: _____

Start Your Day!

Art & Logic Games

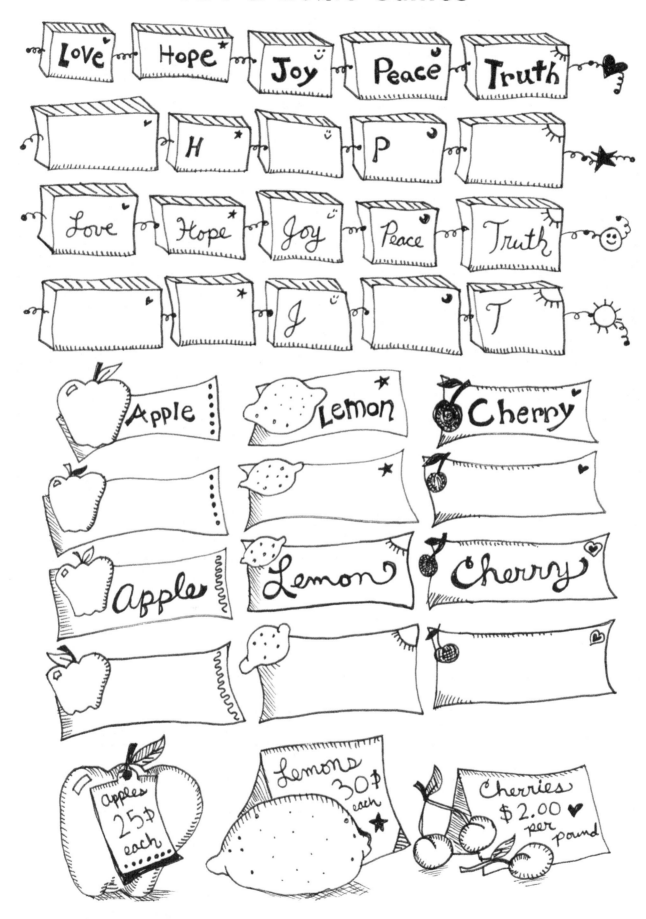

Creative Writing Time
Write a short story about this picture.

Nature Study

Go outside and make a realistic drawing of something you find in nature. Label your drawing.

Reading Time – 1 Hour (Set a Timer)

Choose Four Books - Read from each book for 15 minutes.
Copy important words or pictures from each book here:

Spelling Time Word Hunt

Choose a number between 5 and 12.

#_____

Find 20 words with this many letters.
Write them on this page.

_____   _____
_____   _____
_____   _____
_____   _____
_____   _____
_____   _____
_____   _____
_____   _____
_____   _____
_____   _____

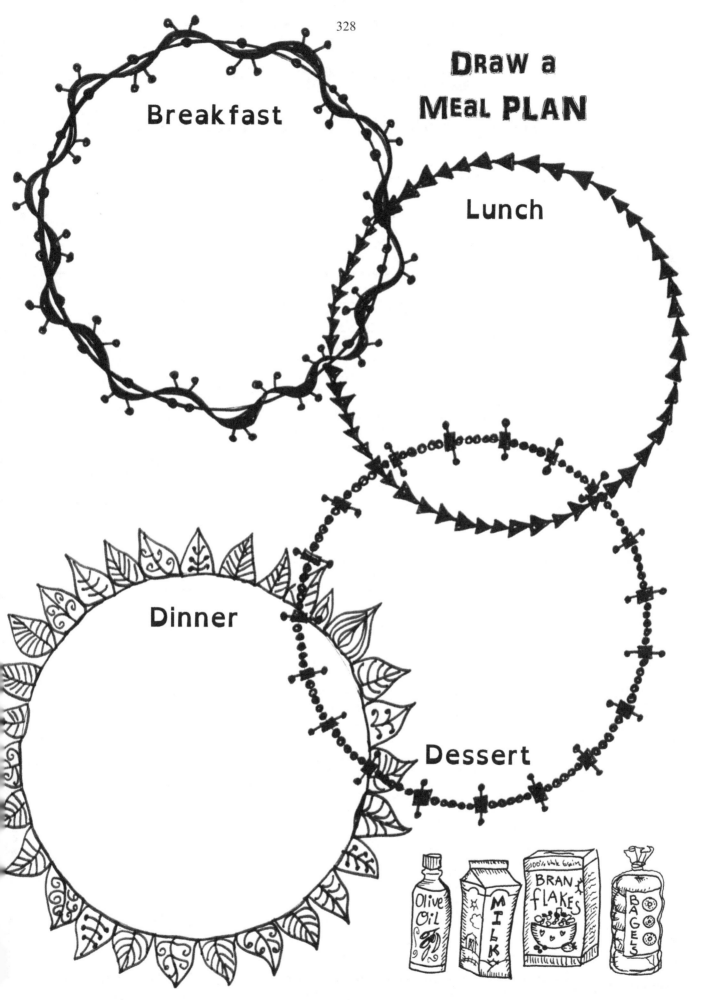

Creative Writing

Stories, Poems, Comics and More.

That's what this page is waiting for!

Animal Quiz

How much do you know about this animal?
Can you draw the animal's habitat, food and enemies?

Date Page - Circle Today's Date

January
February
March
April
May
June
July
August
September
October
November
December

1 2 3 4 5 6
7 8 9 10 11
12 13 14 15
16 17 18 19
20 21 22 23
24 25 26 27
28 29 30 31

MONDAY
TUESDAY
WEDNESDAY
THURSDAY
FRIDAY
SATURDAY
SUNDAY

2020
2021
2022
2023
2024
2025
2026
2027
2028
2029
2030
2031
2032
2033
2034
2035

Write Today's Date: _____

Start Your Day!

COPY A VERSE OR QUOTE

I'M THANKFUL FOR:

TO-DO LIST

Art & Logic Games

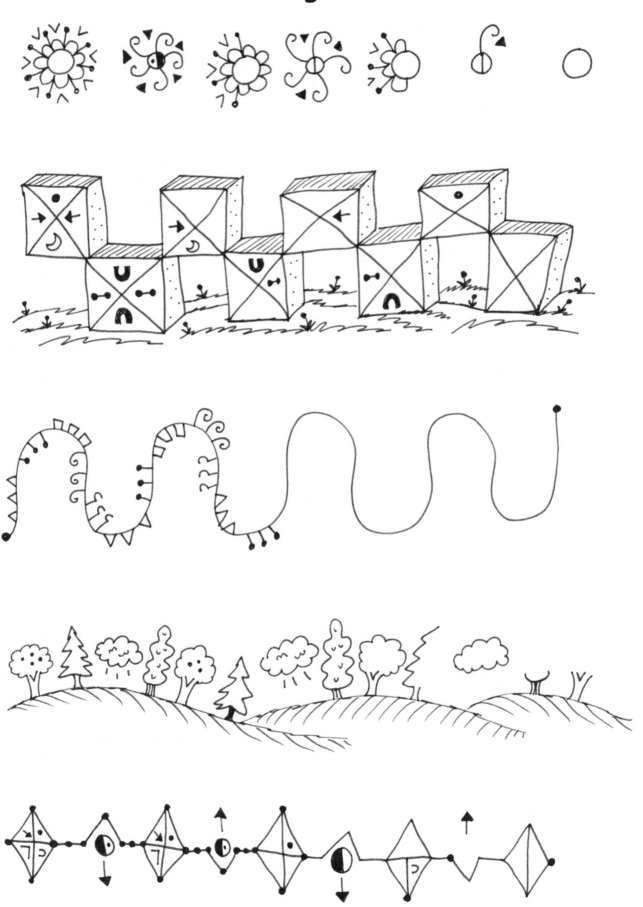

Creative Writing Time
Write a short story about this picture.

Reading Time – 1 Hour (Set a Timer)

Choose Four Books - Read from each book for 15 minutes.
Copy important words or pictures from each book here:

COPYWORK
Copy a paragraph from one of your books.

TITLE: _____

PAGE NUMBER: _____

_____
_____
_____
_____
_____
_____
_____
_____
_____
_____
_____
_____
_____
_____
_____
_____
_____
_____
_____

MATH TIME
USE YOUR MATH BOOK OR ONLINE MATH PROGRAM
Or be creative and design something, like a house!
You could make graphs, maps or geometric designs with this graph paper.

MY MATH RESOURCE: _____
Please note what math book, video or program you are using today.

Animal Quiz

How much do you know about this animal?
Can you draw the animal's habitat, food and enemies?

Creative Writing

Stories, Poems, Comics and More.

That's what this page is waiting for!

Date Page - Circle Today's Date

Write Today's Date:_____

Start Your Day!

Art & Logic Games

Creative Writing Time
Write a short story about this picture.

Nature Study

Go outside and make a realistic drawing of something you find in nature. Label your drawing.

Reading Time – 1 Hour (Set a Timer)

**Choose Four Books - Read from each book for 15 minutes.
Copy important words or pictures from each book here:**

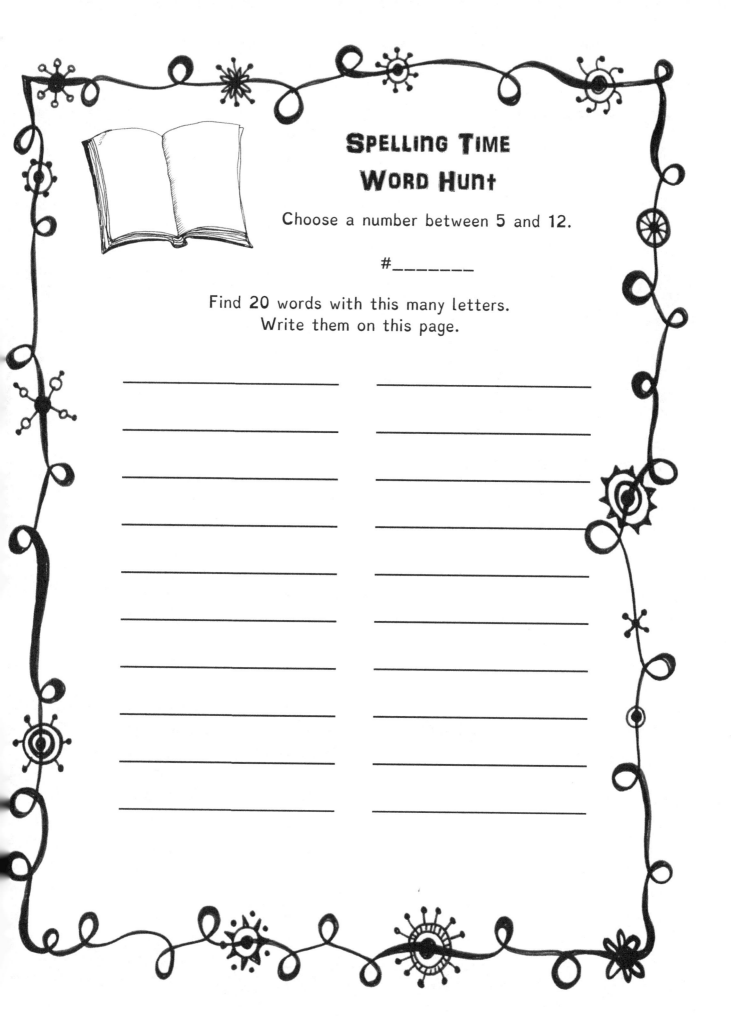

Spelling Time Word Hunt

Choose a number between 5 and 12.

#_____

Find **20** words with this many letters.
Write them on this page.

MATH TIME
USE YOUR MATH BOOK OR ONLINE MATH PROGRAM
Or be creative and design something, like a house!
You could make graphs, maps or geometric designs with this graph paper.

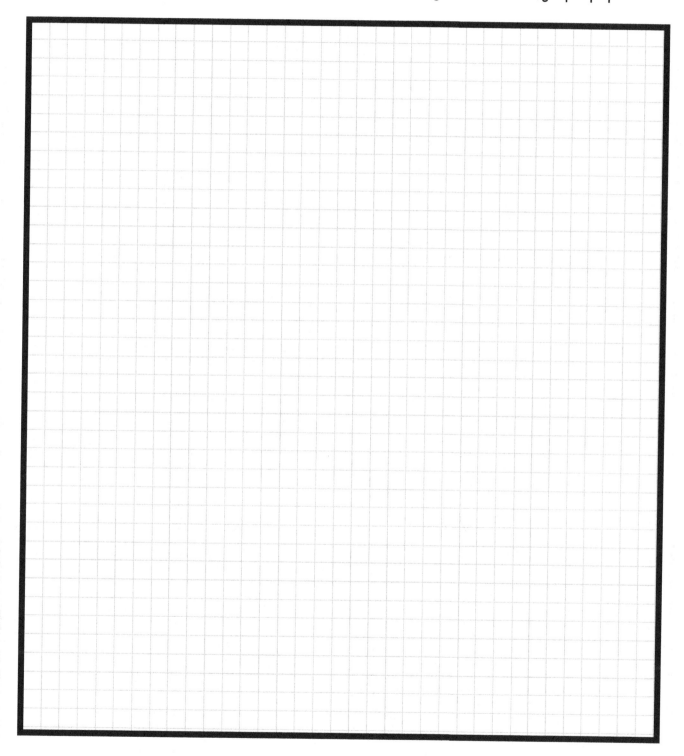

MY MATH RESOURCE: _____
Please note what math book, video or program you are using today.

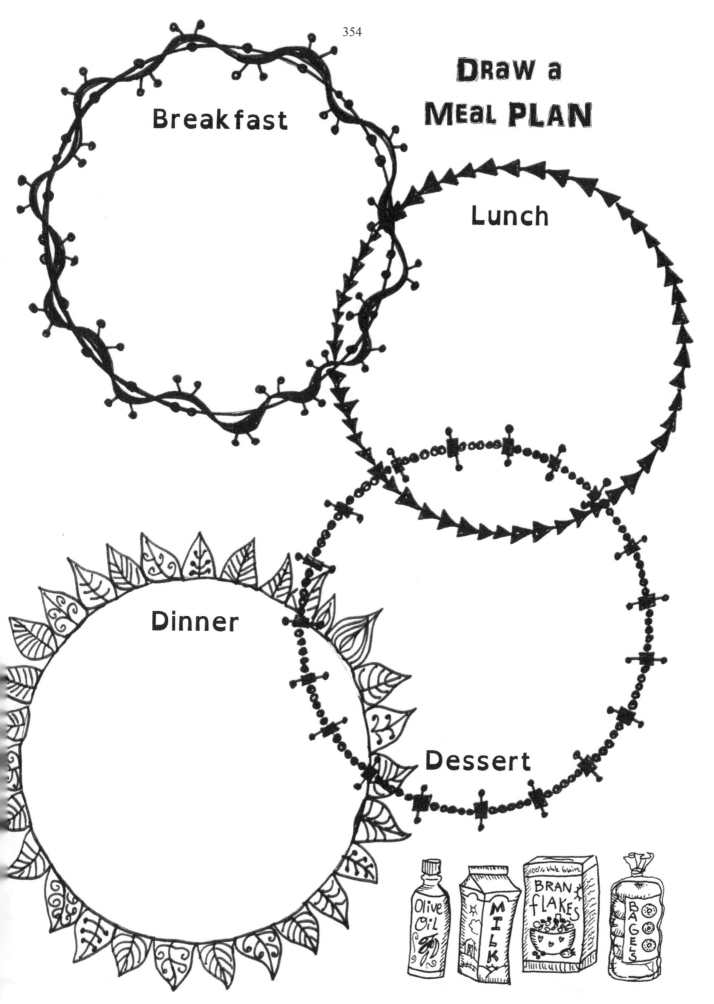

Creative Writing

Stories, Poems, Comics and More.
That's what this page is waiting for!

Date Page - Circle Today's Date

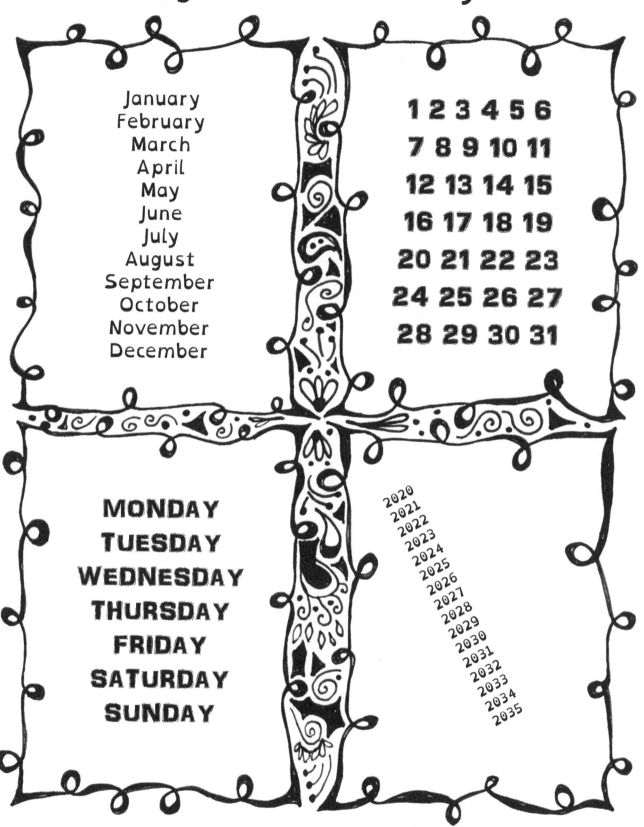

January
February
March
April
May
June
July
August
September
October
November
December

1 2 3 4 5 6
7 8 9 10 11
12 13 14 15
16 17 18 19
20 21 22 23
24 25 26 27
28 29 30 31

MONDAY
TUESDAY
WEDNESDAY
THURSDAY
FRIDAY
SATURDAY
SUNDAY

2020
2021
2022
2023
2024
2025
2026
2027
2028
2029
2030
2031
2032
2033
2034
2035

Write Today's Date:_____

Start Your Day!

Art & Logic Games

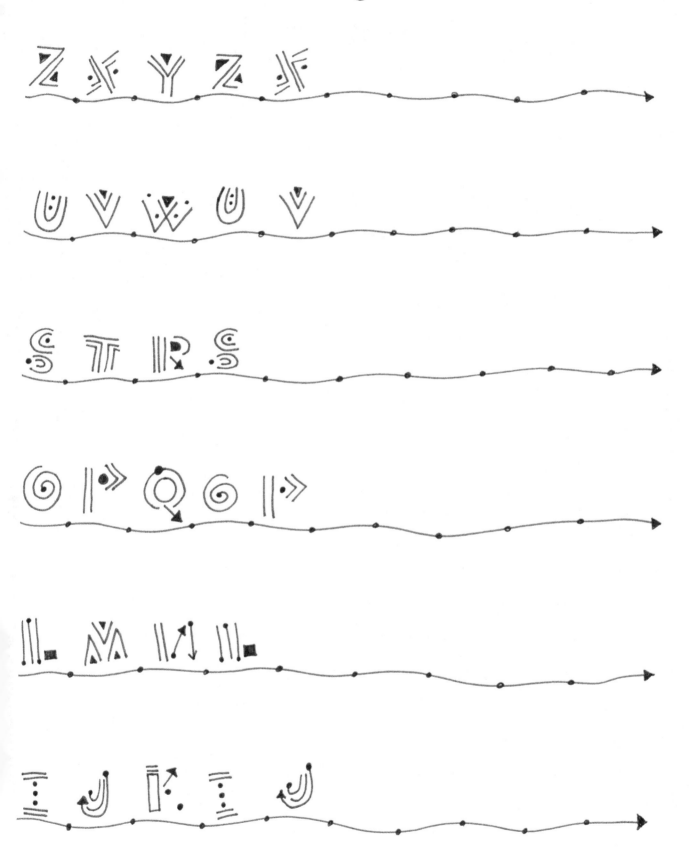

Creative Writing Time
Write a short story about this picture.

Nature Study

Go outside and make a realistic drawing of something you find in nature. Label your drawing.

Reading Time – 1 Hour (Set a Timer)

**Choose Four Books - Read from each book for 15 minutes.
Copy important words or pictures from each book here:**

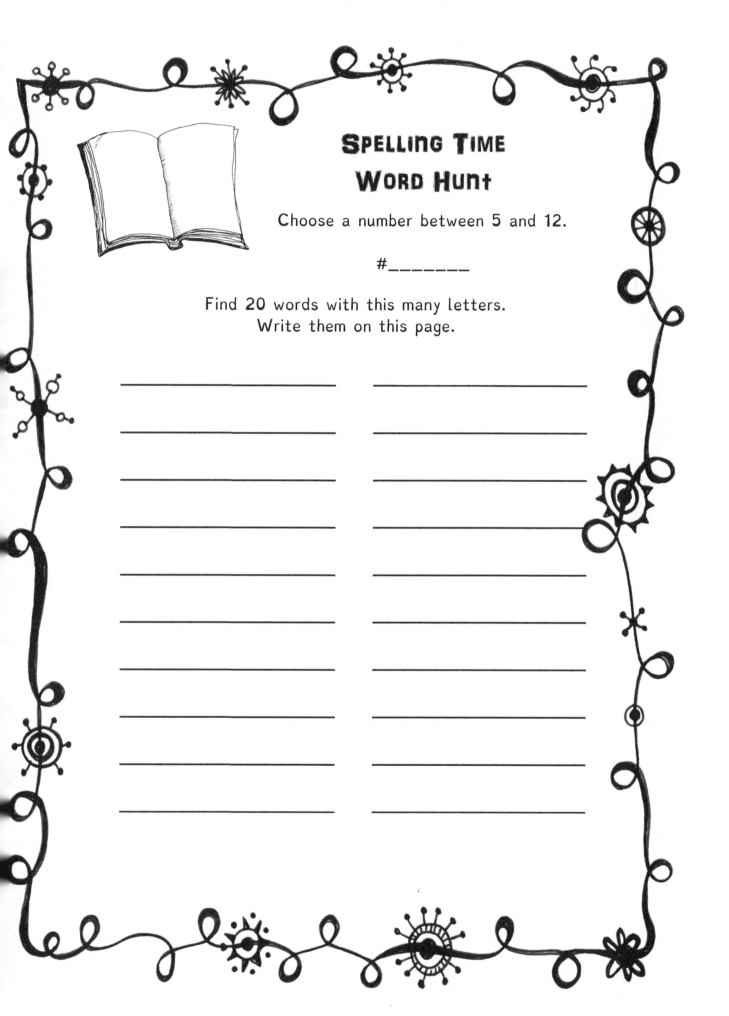
Spelling Time Word Hunt

Choose a number between 5 and 12.

#_____

Find **20** words with this many letters.
Write them on this page.

COPYWORK

Copy a paragraph from one of your books.

TITLE: _____

PAGE NUMBER: _____

MATH TIME
USE YOUR MATH BOOK OR ONLINE MATH PROGRAM
Or be creative and design something, like a house!
You could make graphs, maps or geometric designs with this graph paper.

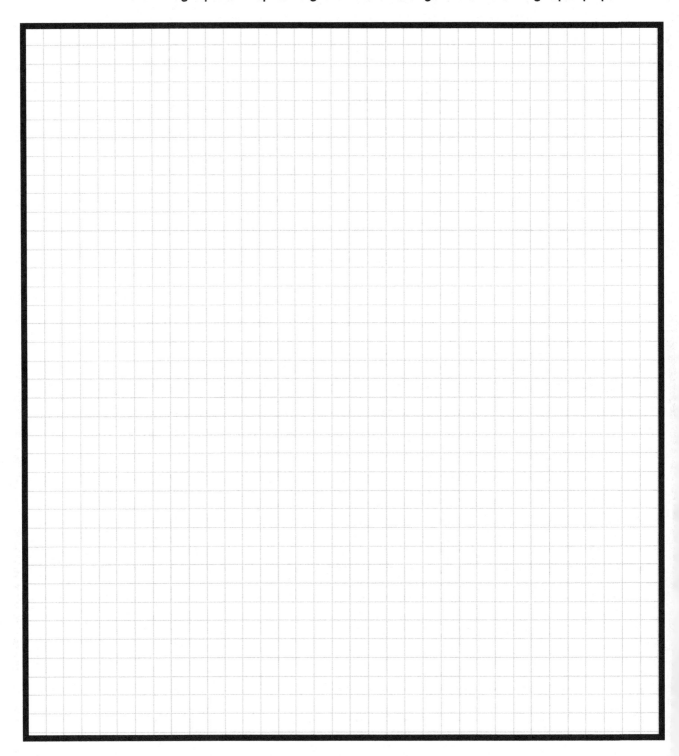

MY MATH RESOURCE: _____
Please note what math book, video or program you are using today.

Creative Writing

Stories, Poems, Comics and More.
That's what this page is waiting for!

Resources Used in Research:

Additional Notes:

Do It Yourself HOMESCHOOL JOURNALS

Copyright Information

Do It YOURSELF Homeschool Journal, and electronic printable downloads are for Home and Family use only. You may make copies of these materials for only the children in your household.

All other uses of this material must be permitted in writing by the Thinking Tree LLC. It is a violation of copyright law to distribute the electronic files or make copies for your friends, associates or students without our permission.

For information on using these materials for businesses, co-ops, summer camps, day camps, daycare, afterschool program, churches, or schools please contact us for licensing.

Contact Us:
The Thinking Tree LLC
617 N. Swope St. Greenfield, IN 46140. United States
317.622.8852 PHONE (Dial +1 outside of the USA)
267.712.7889 FAX
www.DyslexiaGames.com
jbrown@DyslexiaGames.com

Made in United States
Orlando, FL
24 February 2023